THE INITIATION OF
THE WORLD

*Be ye wise as serpents and
harmless as doves*

VERA STANLEY ALDER

The Initiation of
the World

Illustrated by the Author

SAMUEL WEISER, INC.
York Beach, Maine

First American edition in 1972 by
Samuel Weiser, Inc.
Box 612
York Beach, Maine 03910

Fifth printing, 1990

First published in 1939 by
Rider & Co., London, England

ISBN 0-87728-057-6

Printed in the United States of America

Contents

PART TWO

REVIEW OF MATERIAL SCIENCE

Preface

How amazing it is that an intelligent person can go through the whole of his or her life without being aware of either the existence or the importance of the Ageless Wisdom! That vast body of information known as the Wisdom Teaching, whose import stretches from the meaning and purpose of man himself to the constitution and evolution of the whole Universe, would appear to have existed in all its strength since prehistoric times.

It has been the mainstay of all the great early civilisations, giving people a sense of evolution, of Plan and of destiny, wonderful to envisage. It has provided the roots for all the great religions, which are thus intrinsically branches of the one tree. A long line of illustrious teachers and leaders has kept the Wisdom alive, running through the murky pattern of materialistic history like Golden Threads; constituting, in fact, a separate underlying Golden History, the true unfoldment of man's inner evolution.

How sad that throughout the Dark or Middle Ages people became so conditioned by the growing materialism that even the existence of this golden wealth, their real heritage, became hidden from them. Today there is a sealed door in most people's minds which may remain closed, even invisible, throughout their lifetime. When my own sealed door suddenly opened my life was transformed from living in purposeless darkness to living in purposeful illumination. The change was astounding and exhilarating. My first thought was for all those others in whose mansion of the mind the door to the Wisdom was still sealed up.

Why was this so? It seemed that this Teaching was mostly to be found in very long and rather abstruse volumes, in which struggling working humanity had but scarce opportunity for research. Surely a very simple summary of this world of inner reality might be of service? To this end I wrote my first book, *The Finding of the Third Eye,* in which I tried to put out just what I myself would have liked to have read many years before, had it been available.

In my second book, *The Initiation of the World,* I have continued along the same lines, indicating the many aspects of the Wisdom and of its relationship to or identity with present-day 'scientific knowledge'. To a newcomer parts of the Wisdom Teaching may seem involved, almost frightening or unnecessary in their vast complicated presentations. But, although our Universe *is* vast and complicated, we possess within ourselves a replica of the whole design and purpose of creation. We are our own key to knowledge. Hence the ancient dictum of MAN KNOW THYSELF! Our sealed door can be opened through the practice of Meditation when once our will to discover is awakened. This book is designed as a guide to the assessment of the wholeness of life and the trend of evolution. It can be used as a reference book to further studies. It is still the barest of outlines, but it may indicate, nevertheless, what there is to know that will give the key to personal attainment and purposeful living.

PART ONE

Review of Spiritual Science

I

Introduction

HAS there ever before been such a dangerous, exciting and eventful period in world history as that which we are passing through today?

The collective achievements of our scientists beggar the imagination. So does the collective suffering of humanity at this time. Will it all prove to be birth-throes from which a new step forward in civilisation will emerge, the dawning of a new and better age? It seems inevitable that something different must and will evolve from the seething, purging maelstrom in which humanity is involving itself. Either annihilation or regeneration!

There are many who fear that the world is moving headlong towards self-destruction, through violence, cruelty and stupidity. Perhaps they do not take into account human reaction, the swing of the pendulum. If cruelty had led to more cruelty, humanity would have become extinct many generations ago. If it had been possible to crush out love, joy of life, religious fervour, patience and hope from the human heart, we should have seen this accomplished in several epochs in history. Evil has had every possible chance for success—it has even sat upon the thrones of the earth, in omnipotence.

Yet humanity goes patiently forward. It suffers every kind of distraction: the softening effect of luxury; the degenerating effect of poverty; the darkness of ignorance; mistaken leaderships; the greedy oppression of profiteers; the cruelty of fanatics; the muddling confusions brought about by all these; and the final obscenity of war.

Any one of these conditions would have rendered a species of animals extinct in a fairly short time. Yet man still goes on. He struggles through it all, gaining ground imperceptibly, steadily. His standards are shifting ever so gently towards the acceptance of humanity as one common brotherhood. The instinct of charity stretches from the home right round the world. Barriers of race, religion and of class are being dissolved by all those who are sufficiently free from tyranny and tyrannical influence to do as they choose, while the tyranny which imposes unfair and unequal racial conditions is also under attack.

There are signs everywhere of efforts to be free from the ruts, inhibitions and conventions in which people used to be so content to vegetate. Many are quietly busy with constructive humanitarian work. Many others are suffering, fighting and dying for things which they are told are right and good. Between these two, the fighters and the servers, the great unheeding masses strive blindly for their own existence, for comfort and for amusement. Yet they too are roused today by the crescendo of the times. Humanity is being stirred to its depths by an unusual urge to self-expression. They strike, they march, they revolt, all around the globe.

What does it all mean? To what is it all tending? Can it be just chance, coincidence, which is turning the tune of life into a roar, and the rhythms of progress into a stampede?

Is humanity going to be confounded and swallowed up in the chaos of its own muddles? Is self-slaughter through war, and self-starvation through economic greeds, to be the final answer to man-made civilisation? The apparent possibility of this is spreading dread among countless helpless people.

Not, however, among all! Interspersed within the public there are many quiet ones, who say little, and do not appear to do any startling things either. But they hold and guard within themselves a knowledge and a vision giving them apparently the clue to much which is happening. They act as a yeast among their fellow men, keeping them, by a subtle influence, from sinking into despair. They are usually students, under some form, of a body of teachings which is sometimes known as the Ageless or Ancient Wisdom, and which has survived throughout the long reaches of history.

Such people believe that we are in the throes of transition from a long Dark Age into a coming New Age which shall see a glorious unfolding and consummation of the latent flower of spirit and wisdom within man and within our earth. They believe that the divine discontent, awakening widespread among men today, is tuning them rapidly up to the point where they will awaken within themselves new qualities, new senses and quite new ambitions. They believe that the great collective being, humanity, is moving rapidly towards a further stage in its development; that it is soon to bring to birth a part of its consciousness hitherto dormant and unknown; and that the reward of this long weary pregnancy and these convulsive birth-throes will be to have the 'Christ-child', the true spiritual faculty, as a part of our conscious heritage here on earth.

This great change and advancement in development has always been known as Initiation, by those who were the guardians of the Ageless Wisdom. In my former book *The Finding of the Third Eye* the barest outline of the history and teachings of the Ancient Wisdom was given. This includes the Plan of Creation and of Evolution on this planet, and in the Universe, and the fundamental spiritual laws, such as the laws of Reincarnation and Karma, of Cause and Effect. The subject is a vast one. It was developed in enormous tomes, commentaries, and archives in many parts of the world. This literature was in the care of the few intelligentsia, mostly the priesthood. The knowledge of its existence was the greatest thing in the lives of all early civilisations. During successive wars and invasions the archives were destroyed or hidden. Humanity moved forwards into a long Dark Age, during which bigotry and superstition veiled the shining truths. Later there came a reaction against such thraldom, which resulted in the beginnings of the scientific age. Men went to the other extreme. They refused to accept anything which could not be *proved* in materialistic fashion.

Both the way of superstition and bigotry, and the way of materialistic science, have proved insufficient to create a happy and successful world civilisation. Instead they have produced wars innumerable, disaster and chaos, poverty, soil erosion and disease. No one can be content with the state of the world as it is today. It is obvious, even to the unthinking person, that something very vital is lacking in our power to deal with our own lives, both singly and collectively. This lack must surely be due to ignorance, and ignorance must be due to wrong education. In order to prepare for a better type of civilisation, education must be remodelled—but in what way? What is wrong with our thinking?

Scientists say that the average intelligent man uses only a fraction of his brain-cells. Which fraction does he use, and what kind of thinking could he accomplish with the unused remainder? It seems that this muddled world will be put right only when a sufficient number of people learn how to think in such a manner as to be able to put it right! There is surely no other solution. Organised, creative and constructive thinking is the crying need of today. But on what should it be founded? On what foundation were the geniuses of the past produced?

The orthodox history books on which you and I were reared consisted of a long recital of unending wars, invasions, intrigues, oppressions; periods of empire-building followed by periods of luxury followed by periods of decadence and final eclipse. These histories, put out with pride by every country, seem blandly to ignore the fact that all the great religions explicitly forbid violence, oppression, injustice, theft and exploitation. In defiance of their own religions they extol warfare with all its horrors, and speak with pride of all conquests (thefts with violence). What sort of an education is this? It is surely nothing but a preparation for suicide, for 'he who lives by the sword shall perish by the sword'.

So much for orthodox history! But there is another kind of history for us to explore, a *golden history* which holds the key to a glorious future unfoldment. It is that which we are going to piece together in this book.

2

How Giant Intellects are Built

I F we take a survey of the long history of man's intellectual development, certain giants tower like lighthouses above their brothers. They stand forth from all periods of history, explaining the mysteries of life, showing the way, and giving us the laws and the rules of the game of living. Though living thousands of years and thousands of miles apart there is much resemblance in their teaching, in their types of brain and their preferences and methods in study.

Let us see where the resemblances come in between most of these men, as well as many others of the same type whom we will consider later. They all had recourse to higher mathematics or symbolical numbers, by means of which they either obtained the clues to their knowledge or developed their mentalities to the point where they were able to obtain it in some other way. Pythagoras said: 'God geometrises.' He and other giant intellects have realised that the world is created upon a system of exact vibrations, patterns, symbols and dimensions, and that through a study of these numbered vibrations and rays, the symbols of the way in which they intersect to form certain shapes, and the different grades of matter which their varied frequencies precipitate, an understanding of the created world, its trend, purpose and the great Consciousness behind it can be acquired and utilised. Big intellects have always been interested in the purpose of creation, the reason for all created forms and their destiny, the mighty hidden forces, and designs which lie back of it all, and just beyond the reach of man's average physical senses. In turning their minds away from petty personal affairs to concentrate upon these larger issues they have been obliged to bring into action *various latent brain-cells* which are not of use for everyday habits of thought. Their brains have thus expanded and changed in character, although in a way not necessarily wholly visible to the ordinary scientist's microscope as we will explain later. The brain contains five times as many physical brain-cells as the average man brings into use. It holds also their counterparts in finer strata of matter which we call the ethers, as well as in all the seven major planes of matter which we studied before.[1] The brain is like a wireless receiver. With practice one can tune it in to any number in the ladder of created vibrations. The brain is a perfect instrument for the use of the will and the mind. That perfect instrument exists *latent* in the head of every average person. But it is neither understood nor used. Most people go about with at the most a fifth of their consciousness operating. They are therefore four-fifths dead all their lives, and this is no exaggeration.

The mental factor, however, is pulling very strongly at humanity today. Its urge is felt and appreciated. Men are ready and anxious to think, to know and to experience the delights of fuller living. Never in history have there been so many words spoken, written, wirelessed—an outpouring of millions of words every day all over the world. People are striving to think and to develop their mentalities. But they do not know how to set about it. They cannot see that which stands in the way. They have no clue yet as to the true methods of obtaining mental growth. In these chapters we will point the way to those methods, which are our heritage from a rich past.

[1] See *The Finding of the Third Eye.*

Within every average human brain lies the potentiality of greatness, of knowledge and of wisdom supreme. It is the human birthright, the divine legacy. But this hidden waiting wonder is clamped down, shuttered up, imprisoned helplessly away, smothered out of reach by vast layers of inhibitions, thought-patterns, habits, fears, sloth and other rubbish-heaps of decayed, stagnant and static thought-forms. We have studied how this can be cleared away through the age-old methods of self-analysis, meditation, concentration and aspiration.[1] We know how to clear our decks for mental action. We will now consider the types and purposes of all those unused brain-cells, and the way in which we can bring them to life.

If we think about physical things in their outer physical aspect, as we generally do, we use our corresponding mental wireless set of physical brain-cells. If we think of the electrical forces and energies working through those physical forms we must bring into play our corresponding etheric brain-cells. If we think in terms of imaginative emotion we use brain-cells not yet visible to material science, which are built of corresponding so-called astral matter. If we think in the sphere of mental matter we must use a still subtler type of brain-cell. If we wish to think in terms of higher mathematics and cosmic designs we must be able to bring into action our most subtle mental radio set, formed of matter too delicate to visualise with our present understanding. The type of brain-cell which must be brought into use for this could not tune in to the coarse set of physical-plane vibrations with which we would deal as very ordinary persons in everyday life. It could not register or respond to such things as greedy desire, discontent, gossip and dislike, which would be foreign substance to it. But just as the seven planes of creation dwell within and permeate each other, so the various grades of brain-cells dwell within and permeate each other. The force

See *The Finding of the Third Eye*.

which feeds the one does so at the expense of its higher or lower counterparts.

In this way, as one develops and uses the higher cells in investigating the realms of wisdom and understanding, their counterparts in lower-plane matter are atrophied or absorbed or transmuted by the higher vibration. The whole mentality steps up to a grander, more powerful and broader capacity.

Higher mathematics, metaphysics and philosophy have always been valued and used by those of giant intellect. They constitute the science of the invisible, the science of causes as opposed to the material science which deals with effects. Today, at the close of the long age of separatism, we find a big cleavage and many little cleavages in the world's accumulation of knowledge. The big cleavage occurs between so-called spiritual knowledge and so-called material science.

The little cleavages occur everywhere between every art —science, therapeutics, religion, sect and system.

All these barriers of words, labels, communities and habits are holding men apart from each other and from a true understanding and perspective of life and from their own inner, potent selves.

Man must learn to take the largest possible view of life, instead of, as now, the most restricted. According to the size of his mental horizon so will the size of his power be. This is a significant truth, worthy of careful consideration.

The enlarging of a man's scope can be brought about only by the breaking down of barriers, the resolving of cleavages, the fostering of inclusiveness instead of exclusiveness. In the following chapters we will begin this process of barrier-breaking, the bringing of all knowledge and all striving under one banner. We will begin by tackling the big main existing cleavage, and the smaller ones will take their place in our argument of their own accord.

The biggest cleavage of the present day is that existing in.

men's outlook between the so-called spiritual and the so-
called material sciences. These two aspects of the one life
have grown gradually apart during the past hundreds of
years under the influence of the Dark Age. Now that we are
coming out of that period into the Aquarian or Light Age,
these two facets of life will come together in man's comprehension once more. According to the speed with which this
takes place, so will be the speed of the coming into birth of
the new civilisation.

Therefore the resolving of this main cleavage is to be the
most important aspect of future education. When the collection of knowledge which is guarded under the label of
'scientific' is recognised to be identical in certain ways with
the collection of doctrines which is guarded under the label
of 'spiritual', and it is found that the two dovetail completely
and combine with each other to form a perfect and illuminating whole, then we will have at last a Key-Science, a Master-
Science, which will give the answer to all riddles and the
clue to the attainment of man's birthright and glorious destiny.

In this book we will try to indicate the keys to the truths
underlying this statement, and provide a sufficient foundation with which the reader can begin the future master
education for himself. We will outline the fundamentals of
the spiritual sciences, setting them forth as clearly as words
will permit. Whether any one religious presentation of life is
believed in, or none, is of no importance. The fact remains
that it is impossible to think about or visualise the picture
given without bringing to life brain-cells *which can be roused
in no other way*, and thereby expanding the brain so that it
can take in things which would have been incomprehensible and uncongenial to it before. Merely as an experiment
this is worth trying. We have already seen that the original
'religion', or spiritual science, which dates from the dawn of
history, and upon whose deeply hidden roots all other great

religions were founded, still exists for the seeker, and is named the Ageless Wisdom, or the 'Light'. It originated in the days when 'material science' and 'spiritual science' were known to be one and inseparable, and were treated as such.

During the long Dark Age, in which separatism reigned, religion itself, as it crystallised into orthodoxy, became separated from its own source. Separation also grew between spiritual belief, scientific knowledge, psychology, medicine and education. Divorced from their one root, the Ageless Wisdom with its fundamental spiritual Laws, the arts and sciences and religions became steadily more materialistic, more separatist, and more distrustful of each other. Education became conditioned into an orthodox convenience. Instead of being designed to bring out the wonderful potentialities of man himself, as a Divine instrument, he was treated merely as a useful business, commercial or agricultural asset. His possibilities as a man, and as a Son of God, were left to look after themselves; in fact they were unpopular because they might interfere with current social requirements. After generations of such conditioning humanity quite forgot the existence of its own tremendous spiritual birthright. This will have to be learnt all over again with the dawning of the new Aquarian Age, the Age of Man.

The first signs of this dawning arrived during the last century. Certain superminds had the task of giving out the Ageless Wisdom once more to humanity. Little by little a body of teachings took shape and various groups collected around it. These superminds came to be known as the Masters of the Wisdom, those elder brothers of mankind who had matriculated into spiritual adulthood and power through the training of the Ageless Wisdom. The time had come for them to select and inspire and teach the Wisdom to those who could respond to them. One of those selected was Helena P. Blavatsky. Under the influence of the Masters, she wrote the famous *Secret Doctrine* and other books, which became the foundation of the group known as the Theosophists.

Around similar teachings the Rosicrucian groups, the Christian Scientists, the Anthroposophists, the Bahais, and many others of varying qualities came into being in rapid succession.

However, there was more to come. Another gifted writer, Alice Bailey, was chosen to continue the message as first given out to the Theosophists. Once more, under the direction of the same Masters of the Wisdom, a further body of teaching was released, this time very practical in nature. Not only did it amplify the Ageless Wisdom, clarifying its position in regard to both Buddhism and Christianity; but it outlined the whole trend of evolution, applying it both to present and future events. Furthermore, explicit training was given for all aspirants at their various stages of development.

Under the dictation of the Master of the Wisdom, Djwhal Khul, Alice Bailey wrote over a score of lengthy books. Thus a wonderful heritage has been presented to posterity for the building of the future Golden Age, both in regard to information and to instruction. Meanwhile, most of humanity is ignorant of the very existence of any such teaching, either ancient or modern. Tired and hard-pressed, bewildered by a black-and-white world in which good and evil seem inextricably mixed, poisoned and stupefied by wrong living habits of every kind, humanity has hardly the intellect or the time for studious reading, or for self-training and self-analysis in all its ramifications. It is therefore in danger of missing the joy, enlightenment, and the reawakening to a new life and opportunity which such knowledge brings. Short and concise introductions to the vast reaches of both ancient and modern wisdom are urgently needed.

It was the realisation of this need which inspired the writing of *The Finding of the Third Eye*. This was the bare introduction to the theme of 'Man Know Thyself'. In this present book, we can continue to build up our picture from those elementary outlines. The teachings of the Wisdom are, at times, abstruse, because they deal with conditions outside the physical world as we now know it; conditions for which we have as yet no western words. In fact, we sometimes continue to use ancient Sanskrit terms. But the things which the ancients discovered and understood *must* become comprehensible to us once more. Otherwise we will have to conclude that we are going backwards!

3

The Plan of Creation

WE will now continue to summarise the Ageless Wisdom, both as it existed in its original forms, and as it has been amplified by the benefactors of humanity in accordance with successive needs and understanding.

The Ageless Wisdom teaches that the vast galaxy of the heavens which the telescope reveals to us is but the thinnest cross-section of that which is in existence around us. It explains that life as we know it is actually built upon a scale of delicately graded strata of matter, called planes, which interpenetrate and 'feed' each other without losing their respective identity. An entity, whether it be a planet or any other living creature, may exist in a form built of any number of these planes.

It explains that the whole universe, a fraction of which we can observe through the telescope, is one vast organism, held together by one life, living with a consciousness and purpose which it is useless for us to try to understand as yet. This vast organism has its rhythm, motion and organisation into respective parts, such as nebulae and solar systems, which divisions play each their part and contribute each their specialised consciousness to the whole, as all the organs of our own bodies do. Just as the cells in our bodies live, work, reproduce, die and reincarnate soon again as cells of a slightly higher calibre, so do the heavenly cells, the planets and stars, play the same part in relation to the Greater Being, coming into manifestation, living, working, developing, reproducing, dying (or withdrawing from physical manifestation), to return later as stars of a slightly higher development.

That which we call birth, incarnation, death, reincarnation, is simply the movement into and out of a particular octave of vibrations. Human beings contain response-mechanisms for all the different planes within themselves. When they develop these response-mechanisms they will become aware of abundant life upon each of the planes. Not only will they see that each planet or star has its counterpart upon each plane, but they will observe myriads of stars which are at various stages of passing to or from 'physical' incarnation stage, and exist around this earth in invisible forms of varied texture and development. The few stars which we can see, which happen to be in physical bodies at this time, compare in numbers with the invisible stars to the degree that the living humans on the earth today compare with the numbers of those who have lived and died upon its surface.

A faint idea can be had from this of the vast fulness of the universe, and the incapacity of the human mind completely to picture it.

Each differentiation within the vast Universal Being, whether it be a constellation, solar system or plane, is a separate organ or organism, an entity within *the* entity, with its own consciousness and developing life. In the same way each cell within a human form is an entity, with its own consciousness and individuality. The human mind, trapped within the delusion of size and space, may not judge between the consciousness of an atom and that of a planet. Its relative importance is something which he is not in a position to view, or to understand. He can only look at it from his own little standpoint of size—his own little place in an octave which has its own little place on a scale of millions of octaves, with whose existence he can become acquainted only as he vivifies the latent cells in his own brain which correspond to and tune in with them.

Each of the entities within the greatest entity develops itself as a separate and complete organism, although part of the whole. It differentiates within itself into centres and organs, all of which exist in their counterparts of the graded Planes. Each of the differentiations of each of the entities becomes itself an entity, and so the sub-divisions continue and a complicated universe-body is built up.

Finally, at some point in this vast universe where the existences have become small enough for a deeply thinking man to visualise we take our starting-point with one of them, calling him a Deity—*the* Deity, because he is the greatest whom we have the power to imagine.

The ageless wisdom begins by describing this Deity as the 'ONE ABOUT WHOM NAUGHT MAY BE SAID', a being of such wonder and magnitude that we may not as yet presume to think about him. All we know is that this inconceivable entity, who is sometimes called the Absolute, decided for his own inscrutable purpose to create a universe. This universe was created out of his own pregnant, potent atmosphere, which is named Chaos. It was created by the emanating of vibrations. The wonderful and intricate descriptions of how this was done are too lengthy for these pages. We can give only the barest outlines. Through the setting up of varied vibrations and lines of force the seven great Cosmic Planes were formed. These were seven interpenetrating worlds of invisible malleable substance, graded downwards or outwards from the rarest spiritual essence of the First Cosmic Plane to the Seventh Cosmic Plane, which contains the outward manifestation of the created universe.

The Absolute became creative by differentiating himself into three major forces, a triangle issuing forth as Power, The Word, and Motion, or Will, Wisdom and Activity. This triangle differentiated again into the Seven Great Logoi, who embodied and created the Seven Cosmic Planes, each plane being differentiated again into seven sub-planes. It is well to realise that each division in nature is a living organism, ensouled by an entity, whose body of expression it is. This is a difficult idea to get hold of at first, but it is essential to the proper understanding of the Wisdom. Therefore each of the great cosmic planes is the form of a conscious living entity ensouled by a spark from the mind of the Absolute. And as each of the greater entities differentiates again within himself in the act of building creation, he imbues each differentiation with a spark of his own consciousness, which thus ensouls an entity within an entity. So it continues right down the scale, there being nothing in life which does not come under this rule. The whole mineral kingdom, therefore, is an organism, ensouled by an entity which controls and gives it life and consciousness. So is the animal-kingdom, the fire-kingdom and the water-kingdom, all doing their separate work while interpenetrating and supplementing each other. It is the greater or lesser entities behind each manifestation of life whom magicians have always tried to reach and control, believing them to be living consciousnesses working with matter.

The Seven Great Logoi who were brought to life on the First Cosmic Plane differentiated each into seven again, and this differentiation continued right through the Planes until the Seventh and lowest Cosmic Plane was manifested. By this time these Entities, differentiated from the original Seven Great Logoi, were innumerable, and took up their work as the Gods of all the solar systems.

The whole universe of stars is revolving in one direction. Within this greater revolution are lesser revolutions, each made up of a vast company of constellations. It is said that there are forty-nine of these groups, each one containing millions of septenary constellations. A septenary constellation is a group of seven solar systems which all revolve around one centre. To such a group does our solar system belong.

The great occult maxim 'AS ABOVE, SO BELOW' must ever be borne in mind. The major plan upon which the universe is created is repeated in ever-increasing differentiations, reflected downwards into the tiniest atom we can discover, reflected into the composition of man himself. When we consider the Seventh and lowest Great Cosmic Plane, where creation as we can picture it really begins, we find it peopled with the gods of all the solar systems. Each of these gods reflects and repeats the original action of the Absolute. He differentiates himself first into three, the triangle of Will, Wisdom and Activity, or Father, Son and Holy Spirit, or again power, love and intelligence. These three great qualities are again differentiated into seven, by the division of the intelligence quality into four. And we have now our Seven Planetary Logoi reflections of the Seven Great Cosmic Logoi, who were to build our solar system. The solar system is actually the physical body, the outer crystallised sheath of the entity who is its God and who is the greatest Deity to whom we have the power to aspire. We are all minute cells forming the organs and centres of his form, yet we share, if we will make the effort, his mind and nature.

From the spiritual heart of this great God emanates his physical heart, our sun, which beats as a great heart every eleven years and gives life to all the rest of his form.

The Seven Planetary Logoi which he sent out from himself are known by various names: in Christianity as the Seven Spirits before the Throne, and by esotericists as the Seven Rays. They each built a physical body, which is one of the planets of the solar system. These spirits work, develop and evolve together, affecting each other physically with their radiations, and seeking to fulfil the purpose of their overlord, the Solar Logos. Each of them is differentiated, of course, into seven, and has his counterpart or sheath in each of the seven Planes.

The Planetary Spirit, whose body is this earth, was known as the personal God of mankind, the 'jealous' God, Jehovah, the one whom primitive mankind could most easily understand and reach. Only as man advances and broadens in outlook does he appreciate the one God over all, the God of Love, the Sungod, Logos of our solar system. Later he will reach still further to the entity who ensouls the constellation of seven solar systems, of which ours is one.

Of the Seven Great Cosmic Planes, all of them are beyond the comprehension of man except the lowest, the seventh, which we will now consider. By the lowest I always mean the lowest in rate of vibration, as, of course, they all interpenetrate each other. This is one of the things which we cannot understand until those brain-cells which I mentioned begin to come to life—but there are many who *have* understood them and much more besides, so it can be done.

The Seventh Cosmic Plane is sub-divided again into the seven planes from which our and other solar systems are built. They are:

1. The plane of the Logos, the world of God, his mind
2. The plane of Virgin Spirit, where the differentiation into the triangle takes place. The *Monadic* plane
3. The plane of Atma, the spiritual *Will*
4. The plane of Buddhi, ultimate knowledge or *Intuition*
5. The plane of *Manas*, the mind, divided into the higher (abstract) mind, and the lower concrete mind
6. The plane of astral or emotional matter, the world of desire
7. The physical plane

The physical plane is again sub-divided into seven

DIVISIONS OF THE PHYSICAL PLANE

1 The reflecting ether, memory of nature
2 The light ether, medium of sense perception
3 The life ether, medium for growth, propagation
4 The chemical ether, affecting assimilation and excretion
5 Gases
6 Liquids
7 Solids

Therefore the solid physical world as we see it around us is the expression of the lowest set of vibrations of which we know. It is found in the seventh stratum of matter, of the seventh plane of our solar system; the seven planes of which our solar system is built being sub-divisions of the Seventh Great Cosmic Plane. As the physical plane takes up, being so densely crystallised, infinitely less space than all the rest, this table gives us some idea of its relative size and importance.

The above definitions will show the wealth of 'scientific' metaphysical information available, as a contrast with modern laboured materialistic scientific research. When an amalgamation can be effected between the two, new constructive realisations will be more than probable.

4

Reincarnation

We have summarised the way in which Creation fills space according to the Wisdom. Now let us study the way in which it is said to fill time.

Space was differentiated into seven great major sets of vibrations, the Seven Planes, each of which was sub-divided again and re-divided as we saw.

In the same way Time was differentiated into seven great major pulsations, each of which was sub-divided again into seven, the sub-division continuing *ad infinitum*. These pulsations were like great waves having little waves within them, and they are known in the wisdom language as periods and cycles.

Now, if a universe were thus arranged in regular sets of vibrations, swayed by set time-rhythms, it would be unchangeable, robot and for ever the same. To account for progress we have to bring in another factor. This is the factor of choice, adaptability, individuality—that which has been named free-will. This produces a quality which we call genius, which is the capacity to act in an individual, original way. We see this quality in plants and animals, which adapt and change themselves to suit their environment, and we see it much more clearly marked in mankind. The quality of genius produces a result which certain of the Rosicrucian teaching[1] calls 'Epigenisis'. This means that a continual

[1] See *The Rosicrucian Cosmo-Conception*, by Max Heindal.

modification, evolution or change is always going on. There-fore when the cycle or circle of time passes through a certain physical phase, as it does at regular intervals, we never get an exact repetition of effects. This is because meanwhile Epigenisis has been in action, change and transmutation have been taking place, the physical manifestations are mostly keyed up to a higher vibration than before. So the cycle of time is obliged to pass over on a higher arc, and we do not get a continuous circle—but a spiral. Therefore the great impulse of Time moves in a spiral form and never travels over the same line a second time under the same conditions.

All this is very difficult to picture and to understand with our three-dimensional brains, but as it has already been understood and fully explained by many others, why should we fail?

Time is the positive father-line of force which pushes all things onwards to completion and perfection. Space is the great Mother, the negative strength, cradling within her bosom all that which is to be brought to birth. When the two meet an expression of creation takes place and exudes out-wards through the planes until it finally crystallises in the physical solid plane for a while. There it is strengthened by pressure and friction, developed and individualised, after which it leaves the physical plane (dies) and sinks back through the planes to its original source, *plus* its gained experience and capacity—Epigenisis. There it awaits until the Father-Time comes round once more and pushes it into manifestation again—the same phase of creation, appearing armed with its former experiences, back upon the physical plane among the conditions and vibrations, some of which it had itself brought about. It must either defeat these, neutralise itself with them or succumb to them. So it struggles on until Father-Time sweeps it back again through the Planes.

Such is the process of reincarnation, as it affects solar

system, planet, man, animal, plant and all forms of life. It is one vast continuous process of strengthening, individualising and refining, repeated over and over until the ultimate aim is achieved.

What is this ultimate aim?

We are told that the Gods of the solar systems and planets progress also until they graduate to higher work in higher spheres of which we can form no conception. Their places are thus left vacant and must be filled by those who were once human beings and have striven and progressed until they have qualified to wear the body of a planet or solar system. To thus qualify one must become creative, individual and original. This can be achieved only by fighting one's way out of the blinding, imprisoning depths of physical matter. It was to this end that our earth came into existence. All of its seven bodies are imprisoned and restricted by the seventh physical one, just as all the human spirits moving upon its surface have their subtler bodies imprisoned within a seventh physical one of the same material.

Constellations reincarnate. They move through the planes in and out of physical manifestation at vast periods of time. So do solar systems and planets. Let us consider the reincarnations of our earth. We are told that our earth will have experienced seven major incarnations. Today it will be sufficient to concern ourselves with the present one. As it slowly manifested outwards from the inner planes of higher frequency it took its forms from one after the other of the seven planes of our solar system, until it was in possession of its seven sheaths, globes or bodies, completed finally in the seventh physical one as the earth we know.

We will study its long present period of physical manifestation, in the middle of which we are living today. Having built itself first within the four ethers, it then took gaseous shape, as scientists themselves tell us. It was then brought to birth, cast off from its parent sun, as were the other planets in their respective order. The inner meaning of this was that the Solar Deity had differentiated from within himself at this time the 'Seven Spirits before the Throne,' while creating his own body, the solar system.

Our earth, under the impulse of its ensouling spirit, crystallised still further and became molten liquid. Gradually a crust formed, and the Planetary Spirit found himself finally imprisoned within a physical skin. The same process is undergone by each human monad or individual spark of spirit.

Once our earth was established on the physical plane its life was divided into seven great periods. During these periods, life evolves upon seven great continents. Human beings progress through ensouling seven great successive root-races. These are each sub-divided into seven minor races and so on into further sub-divisions.

We are now living during the middle of the fourth great period, that is to say that our earth is just past middle age. Some time ago our earth touched its lowest densest expression of physical matter. From then onwards it will enjoy the process of transmutation, becoming ever more etheral and highly potent, until the seven periods of its physical existence are over. Then the Planetary Spirit withdraws Himself from it, just as does human spirit at 'death'. The earth gradually sheds its sheaths through the planes and returns to its source. It goes through phases of development on the inner planes, digests and assimilates the fruits of physical experience, and then begins its return journey outwards again through the planes towards a further physical incarnation, appearing finally to physical eyes as a new planet.

We must try to give up the habit of thinking of the higher planes as being above the others in space. The word 'higher' in this case refers only to higher rates of vibration or frequencies. Space itself has to do with only the lower planes. The planes interpenetrate each other. To move from one to the other it is necessary only to change one's rate of vibration

considerably!—or else to be able to shift one's consciousness
to focus in a different stratum of vibrations. It is like changing one's vibrations from those of the material of the electric
wire to those of the electricity itself. It is this capacity to shift
the consciousness from plane to plane which is the aim of
yoga and most spiritual training. The hidden wonders of the
spheres are discovered not by sailing off into the clouds, but
by withdrawing ever inwards, within and within through
the higher dimensions. These are built quite the opposite
way to space as we know it.

Therefore when a planet begins to 'die', withdrawing
through the planes, it may still occupy the same 'space' in its
subtler sheaths or 'bodies', although invisible to the physical
eyes. There could be planets surrounding us in these (to us)
invisible phases, exercising, nevertheless, a considerable influence upon us with their radiations. Such influence would not
be accounted for by average astrologers or astronomers. This
offers one reason why these sciences must include more
knowledge before they can become really efficient.

Continuing with our study of this particular incarnation
of our earth, we are told that, as it solidified, the human
beings, who were already in existence upon it in ether form,
solidified too, and developed, one by one, the various sense
organs as they were needed. They went through successive
amazing stages, which are all said to be recapitulated within
the human embryo, until they had become recognisable as
men and women, albeit animal-men and animal-women.
This long process of 'descent into matter', which applies to
all forms of life besides the human, is called by the name of
involution. It necessarily took place before evolution could
begin. But the two activities still overlap.

Animal-man continued to develop, much as the higher
animals do today, striving unconsciously towards the future
gift of mind and of an individual soul. Finally there came a
moment which so far has been the greatest in man's history.

He had struggled patiently to the point where his vibrations could house the spark of mind or individuality. Then a tremendous event took place. This even we call 'individualisation'. Man stepped out of the animal kingdom into the human kingdom. Each human being acquired a separate soul or individuality, and the power to use the plane of mind. This great event is said to have taken place about eighteen million years ago. It marks the point where the history of man as *man* can be said to have begun. The word 'man' is derived from the Sanskrit, meaning 'mind'.

The process of involution was now over as far as man was concerned. The 'fall' into matter was complete, the divine spark had descended and been buried within physical substance and the long struggle towards the light was about to begin.

But what of the planet itself and the great Spirit who ensouls it? What is the connection between the planet and mankind? Are men but little queer parasites upon its surface, or have they indeed an intrinsic connection with it?

The Ancient Wisdom has a rather wonderful explanation ready for us on this point. If we turn to the microcosm of the human being as our study, we see that the individual has a brain, which is a physical instrument of the mind, but that the mind (or the cells of the mind) invade the whole body and can concentrate in any part of it. The mind is made of cells built from the matter of the mental plane. They form a mental *body* whose surface stretches out further than the periphery of the physical body, as we saw in *The Finding of the Third Eye*. The brain is really only the switchboard between the mental and physical bodies.

In an analogous manner our Planetary Spirit possesses a physical body, the earth, whose metabolism is largely due to mineral action, as is ours—whose movements are brought about by the play of electrical forces through it, as are ours. As the earth is a living being, we are told that it has a heart and brain within its inner structures. We know that its Spirit is one of the Seven Mighty Spirits before the Throne, a division of the Spirit of the God of our solar system. We have therefore accounted for all except the *mind* of our planet, which, if the analogy with the human being be correct, should stretch a little beyond the surface of its body.

We are told, therefore, that human beings themselves constitute the mind-cells of this planet, and that as they evolve and reincarnate ever to a higher state of development, so the consciousness of the planet is able to grow, and its great Spirit is able to take ever more and more control of it. Through human endeavour the transmutation of the mentality of the planet is taking place. The vibrations of the whole surface of the globe are being raised, until they will reach the point where they fuse with the planetary soul.

We have here the true significance of mind over matter shown forth. The mind and the emotions in man rule his body, alter his metabolism, and cause vital chemical changes and upheavals. Angry moods cause a disease to develop, a poison to be formed, which erupts within or upon the surface of the body. Love and noble aspiration produce actually a nectar within the body which heals and rejuvenates. So it is with the planet on a larger scale. Combined bad thinking, wars, revolutions, greed and racial envy on the part of the human mind-cells of the planet breed a poison within the great body which results in disease—and this manifests as epidemics, volcanoes, earthquakes, angry gales, storms, whirlpools and other destructive disturbances.

It may be asked, perhaps, what part the animal and vegetable kingdoms play in the life of our planet. The subject is too involved to go into here, but a hint may be given. A study of the chemical results upon the earth of vegetable and animal life may show an analogy with some of the functions of microbes, blood corpuscles, hormones, phagocytes and other little bodies within the human being. The Plan of the

Universe repeats and repeats itself on all the planes, and on every scale, but always with variations.

All this seems to be far from our subject—reincarnation. But really it is bringing us nearer to a vision of the whole picture. When, eighteen million years ago, man was individualised, that meant the individualisation of the planetary mind also; it meant that the earth had arrived at the age which corresponds to a human being's twenty-first year, and had become 'adult'. The three first great periods of this planetary incarnation were over and the fourth (the one in which we are still living) had begun.

During the first period the first great root-race lived—quite differently in most ways from ourselves. They have been given the name of the Adamic race. Because of the existing composition of the earth they could be incorporated only in the density of astral bodies. During the second period the second great root-race was established. This was called the Hyperborean race, functioning in bodies of etheric matter, and inhabiting the Hyperborean Land. During the third period the third great root-race was established upon the continent of Lemuria, and called the Lemurians. This name comes from the animals, the Lemurs, whose ancestors were supposed to have first existed there. The Lemurian root-race ran its long course. It developed through its seven sub-races into the completely human type, which finally became individualised as divine human beings, eighteen million years ago. It is said that the few remaining remnants of the Lemurian root-race comprise the present Australian aborigines and the Hottontots. They will inevitably soon die out.

The fourth great period saw the birth and development of the fourth root-race, the Atlanteans, dwelling upon the continent of Atlantis. They evolved to a wonderful point in civilisation in their time. But they abused their knowledge, and finally lived so wickedly that they caused a 'disease' in

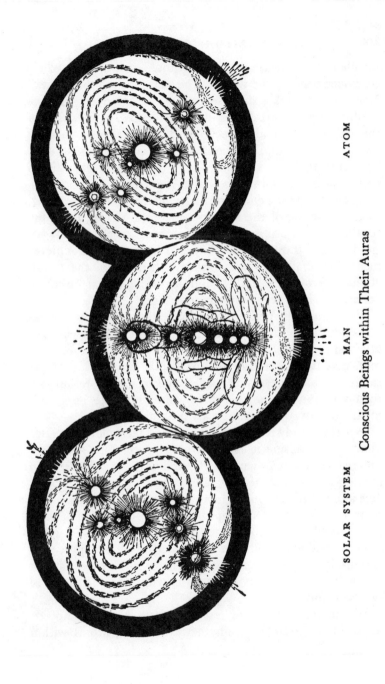

SOLAR SYSTEM   MAN   ATOM

Conscious Beings within Their Auras

the planetary body resulting in a gradual sinking of the whole continent beneath the waters. The story of the Flood and of Noah and the Ark is supposed to describe this event, and the gradual emigration, during the subsidences, of branches of the Atlanteans in all directions. They were said to have founded Egyptian, Peruvian, Druidic and other cultures. The present Tartars, Chinese and Mongolians are said to represent the last sub-races of the Atlanteans.

The fifth great period, during which we are now living, saw the coming of the fifth root-race, the Aryan, upon the continent of Europe. Each great race enjoys finally its 'golden age', producing the flower o fits particular achievement. We shall soon come into the heritage of the Aryan golden age, of the splendour and surprise of which we can as yet have no idea, the great Aquarian Age.

Two other long periods, bringing to flower two more great root-races, lie in the future. By that time the human will have attained divinity, the planetary mind will have merged with soul, and the purpose of this particular incarnation of the earth will have been achieved. Physical manifestation will then cease for a time. This globe will disintegrate, its ensouling life withdrawing to the great 'Within'.

When we study reincarnation we must take a long-distance view of it, realising it as a universal process. An atom is a unit which has its own quality and activity, vibrates and revolves at its own measure, and coheres around a nucleus. The atom of the chemist is like a miniature solar system. The solar system itself is a giant atom. From one point of view man himself is an atom. Each of the planes is also a great atom, containing, as it does, the 'nucleus' of the Spirit who ensouls it, the 'electrons' or subsidiary entities who work within it, its own quality and activity, vibration and spherical revolving form.

We can think of the universe, therefore, as being composed all of atoms, from the minute to the great, atoms within atoms, in infinite complexity. Each one of these atoms incarnates, lives for its allotted spell, disincarnates, enjoys a period of 'rest', and then reincarnates again. It continues this process within the particular species of atom to which it belongs, until it has exhausted all that there is to be learnt and experienced within the confines of that species. It has then 'graduated' in that particular 'class'. The next time it incarnates we find it in the lowest class in a species of higher quality altogether, for which its vibration had become sufficiently heightened.

Each of the succeeding great root-races is of superior quality to the former one, of higher vibration, finer tissue, greater sensitivity. When a man had 'graduated', after many aeons, out of the first root-race he was able to incarnate into the second root-race, and so on. Certain of these lagged very much in their progress, and are still rounding off that particular phase of experience in one of the remnants of the earliest races. When they have all completed that stage of development these remnants will die out. By the same token certain egos who have made rapid progress have already been able to take incarnations in bodies of the coming sub-race of the next great root-race. They move amongst us, think differently from ourselves and are much more highly sensitised in certain ways. But unless we know exactly what we are looking for we shall not discover them. America will be the continent upon which this future race will finally flower, it is said.

So the great chain of reincarnating evolution moves ever forward, upwards in frequency of vibration, onwards in capacity and experience. Side by side with the human evolutionary tide of life are many others—the mineral, the vegetable, the animal, and the angel or devic. When the combined consciousness of the mineral kingdom has 'graduated' and achieved liberation from that school of training it will reincarnate into the animal kingdom (or its equivalent at that time). When the animal kingdom has achieved liberation it will move up into the human kingdom (as it will exist at that far-future date). The fourth kingdom in nature, the human kingdom, will graduate into the fifth or spiritual kingdom. This is the consummation to which we are rapidly approaching today.

Each of these kingdoms helps to transmute the one below and is helped by the one above. Each atom in the universe, great and small alike, is treading the Path of Attainment, the Way of Initiation. Those whom we are in the habit of speaking of as Initiates and Adepts are certain men who have elected to speed up their progress by hard discipline and suffering, with the object of being later in a position to help the weaker ones upon the Path, and assist Those far above them in achievement. The sole aim and object of all genuinely great ones is service—not personal achievement or reward.

Before we leave the subject of reincarnation let us consider one more explanation, from the Ageless Wisdom, of its workings. It is said that each of the seven bodies built of the seven plane atoms, of which each man is composed, contains one particular atom which is called the 'seed-atom'. In this all the experience gained is stored up. After death all the atoms in all the bodies disintegrate and are scattered abroad, but the seed-atom is preserved intact until the ego is ready for a further incarnation. The ego pushes outwards through the planes, draws to it the seed-atom of its former mental body and attracts vibrationally atoms of similar type to build the mental body once more. The ego also draws to it its former seed-atoms of both the astral and physical body. So it is able to build once more a framework intrinsically suitable and karmically adaptable, carrying on, so to speak, from where it left off before. Planets and other living entities have their seed-atoms also. Just as the tiny seed of a flower holds within it the accumulated growth and adaptability, the complete form, design and plan of the plant, so do these seed-atoms, built of matter of the less visible planes, contain also a comprehensive storehouse within their tiny magic periphery.

It is through these seed-atoms that the process of reincarnation which rules the whole universe is able successfully to be carried forward.

In this chapter we have pieced together the various postulates or teachings which have existed from the most ancient times, and have also been elaborated by the advanced minds of this century. As all these teachings overlap it is impossible to give fair credit where credit is due. On the contrary, our object in this book is to give an overall picture of the grand Design of Evolution as it has been given to man throughout his history. The reader can then judge of its feasibility through his own degree of intuition.

The vast world-wide accumulations of writings on these subjects contain necessarily certain seeming contradictions. It must be remembered that they have been given out to meet varied stages of understanding. Truth is an ever-flowing tide. It can only flow through an open mind, and only a continually moving spirit can keep up with it. Have we such a 'moving spirit' and can we face up to the newest teaching about the Rays?

5

The Rays

THE average human being is apt to think of unseen entities in terms of his own form, or of other forms with which he is familiar. To his God he has always given a human form, or else the shape of some familiar animal. It is natural that this should be so, especially when, for instance, man has been told that he is made in the image of God. Having a physically focused consciousness, he promptly thinks of his own *physical* form in this connection, and visualises God in this aspect. But man's physical form is only the final densest crystallised little stratum of himself. It is not his permanent or intrinsic self—it is his instrument. His etheric body, or framework, stretches a little beyond the surface of his physical body, although it follows the same form. His mental body stretches out still further and has a form more of an oval shape.[1] His aura and his astral body stretch out further still and the whole is seen as a globe of fine, rapidly moving, iridescent coloured particles of subtle matter. This globe rotates around the vital centres in man's body, its particles flowing outwards from these centres, sweeping round, eddying and swirling, and returning again to the centres. Therefore man, seen as a whole, *is* a rotating spherical form, with a living nucleus, the heart, and various vital living centres which might be thought of as his electrons. Considered thus, man's resemblance to either a planet or an atom becomes more conceivable.

[1] See *The Finding of the Third Eye*.

It is said that when man first took form upon this planet his body was spherical, and that before he finally leaves it he will be completely spherical once more, but with a great difference. At the beginning his consciousness was exterior and subjective as is that of the animal. At the end it will be interior, dynamic and creative. The spherical form is said to be the ideal one from many points of view.

The object of these preliminary remarks is to try to loosen the mental attitude as to the forms in which conscious entities may dwell, function and develop. If a man had never seen a snake he would not believe that such rapid movement could be achieved by a creature without legs or limbs to help itself. In the same way, unless he has second sight and can observe for himself, he cannot believe that beings can exist in cohesive 'solid' form which is not registered by the physical senses. Nor can he conceive how such a being as that inhabiting a planet can have a consciousness, a purpose, can 'see' without the human type of eye, or feel without the human type of sense organs.

The human being stands midway in a vast scale of conscious evolving entities, some at a lower stage and some at a higher stage of development than himself. The consciousness of the Deity of our solar system is made up of the consciousness of all of these, as well as of man.

Bearing this in mind, we can now touch upon the vast and complex subject of the Rays.

We know that a solar system is composed of a sun holding its planets revolving around it in its sphere of attraction. We learn from the Ageless Wisdom that a constellation is formed of two or more solar systems, held together by mutual attraction between their suns. The constellation to which our solar system belongs is composed of seven solar systems, which form the body and ensoul the life of the greatest Deity of whom we may think: the 'ONE ABOUT WHOM NAUGHT MAY BE SAID'. This Deity, in whose organism we live and have our being, elected to create his physical form and manifestation in terms of a division into seven. Therefore from the vortex of his creative primal energy he issued forth seven great breaths—or Rays. These are seven differentiations of intelligent creative energy. They colour and express all creation as it exists within our constellation. Seven mighty Logoi or Spirits ensouled these Rays, who built each a solar system as his body of manifestation. One of these is the Logos of our own solar system, our own Divine God. He is therefore swept into being *on* one of the Major Seven Rays (the Second one). He repeats the divine creative process, dividing the Ray again into Seven with which to build his own body, our solar system, which is therefore conditioned *by the Seven subsidiary Rays of the Second of the major Cosmic Rays*. The Seven Spirits before the Throne (our seven planetary Logoi) each ensouled a Ray and took incarnation within one of the seven sacred planets of our solar system.

We will now consider the Seven Rays of our solar system, remembering always that they are a repetition on a smaller scale of a greater manifestation. Our solar Deity created his form of expression by dividing his Divine Self from the One into the Three, the primary three which occur before all manifestation. These three were Spirit, Soul and Body, named in the case of our Deity as Will, Wisdom and Activity respectively—or Father, Son and Holy Spirit.

The life of the Deity before he began to build his form was expressed as white spiritual light. He had to divide this great Ray of Light (by means of which he emanated from a greater Deity still), splitting it up into the three great Primary Rays of this solar system, the Red Ray (Will), the Blue Ray (Love-Wisdom) and the Yellow Ray (Intelligent Activity).

These three Major Rays embodied the three principal facets of the creative consciousness of the Deity. They were his three first breaths, with which he spoke, and is still speaking, the *Word* of creation. Everything in the universe exists fundamentally upon one of these Breaths or Rays, and partakes in its other aspects of the life of the other two Rays.

The First Ray, the Red Ray, Will, is the expression and embodiment of the male positive aspect of the Ego of our solar Logos or Deity.

The Second Ray, the Blue Ray, Love-Wisdom, is the expression and embodiment of the Soul, the heart-aspect, of our solar Logos.

The Third Ray, the Yellow Ray, Intelligent Activity, is the expression and embodiment of the Body, the Manifesting Aspect, the activity of matter, in which the Son immerses himself in order to develop his own qualities of creative deity, and, having done so, return (the Prodigal) back into the divine spheres of his Father once more.[1]

In charge of the Third Ray, therefore, is the tremendous task of producing the body, brain and activities of the solar system. To perform this task it emanates four further Rays from its own powers, and thus the Seven Rays come into being. There are, then, the major primary rays of red, blue and yellow, the subsidiary rays of orange, green and violet, and the synthesising ray of indigo, in which the other colours all meet and blend. This great Cosmic manifestation is repeated for us by our little earthly rainbow, when the white light of the sun is sub-divided into these seven colours before our eyes.

Ray Four expresses the goal to which the created physical world is struggling—harmony. This harmony can only be attained and appreciated through learning balance, and this is reached through conflict, leading finally to balance, harmony, beauty and intuition. Therefore this Ray gives the suffering and stress which produces art in many forms, and leads finally to intuition or pure reason. It is said that this

[1] See *A Treatise on the Seven Rays*, by Alice A. Bailey.

Ray uses as its body of physical expression the planet Mercury, which has a very high vibration indeed.

Ray Five is the ray of concrete knowledge or science, by means of which man's mind gradually stabilises his emotions and reaches to an understanding of the plan of creation. Curious as it may seem, the physical expression of this Ray is said to be the planet Venus.

Ray Six is the ray of idealism and devotion, producing that one-pointedness or fanaticism which enables humanity to persevere to its goal through every conceivable obstacle. This Ray, which is in a certain sense the fighting ray, ensouls the planet Mars.

Ray Seven governs Ceremonial Order, or Magic, giving us those laws, rhythms and designs which hold and evolve creation, and which when understood and wielded by man make of him a 'magician'. This Ray ensouls our moon, whose significance we shall consider later.

Every aspect, form, attribute and movement in life is brought about by the influence of the Rays. Everything in existence belongs primarily—that is to say its soul is located—on one of the three major Rays, while its astral, mental and physical parts are governed and built by the combined influence of other Rays. The complexity and vastness of the subject of the Rays can thus be imagined. I can do no more at this time than very briefly indicate what there is to be known about them. Although all the Rays are always in power *latently,* they do have definite periods of incarnation or activity. A Ray's influence will sweep outwards into physical life, incarnate for a period of many hundred years, and produce a particular phase either of development in the animal or mineral or plant worlds, or in the human world. In the latter it may bring out a period of art, science, war, religion or constructiveness, according to the Ray in question.

Each great root-race (and each branch race) belongs to its Rays, having its soul-ray (or esoteric ray) and its personality ray (or exoteric ray). The same applies to each man and each conscious being. In the process of evolution attention is first concentrated in the personality. When its complexities (built into it by combined rays) are finally mastered and co-ordinated a man appears with a dynamic and powerful personality, very ego-centric. There is then a battle between the soul and the personality, which is long, fierce and difficult. Finally and inevitably the soul wins, its Ray takes full control, and one of the initiations has been achieved. The man then continues his progress under soul-domination and illumination. The final and last phase (on this earth) is for him to discover his Spirit and the Ray to which it belongs. He then recognises his own Deity, the Lord of his Monadic or spiritual Ray. This constitutes a further great Initiation. Man has then controlled and perfected all his bodies and subdued them to the rule of spirit and the fusion with spirit. He has become the perfect man, God in human form. He therefore has nothing further to learn by incarnating on this earth. He need do so no more, unless he chooses, as certain great Spirits have done, to return to its restricting surface in order to help his fellow men. Or he may prefer other kinds of work, such as to fit himself, by further Initiations, to become Lord of a minor ray or a planet, or some such task of which we can have no real conception.

The fundamental way in which to understand a human being, therefore, is to get to know upon which Rays are his soul, and his personality, and further upon which rays are his physical, astral and mental bodies, which go to make up that personality. One can then better understand the conflicts within the whole, the super-conscious direction of the man's life, and the stage to which co-ordination and co-operation has so far reached. Besides this a man is influenced by the Ray of his particular nation, and of his race. He is influenced by the particular stage of evolution (from the Ray point of view) of our Planetary Deity (who is not one of the Ray Spirits), of his karma, and the particular Initiation to which he is now striving. Man is also naturally influenced by the present evolutionary activity of our Solar Logos, and of the other six Solar Logoi which make up our constellation, and finally by the consciousness of the Logos of our constellation himself, the "ONE 'ABOUT WHOM NAUGHT MAY BE SAID' ".

A reflection on these things gives much illumination as to the many 'outside' influences and forces which seem to sway man's destinies and swing him into currents over which he seems to have no control. The subject is one which will not be properly understood or put to use for many generations to come. But it is said that it will finally constitute the foundations of future psychology, and help man safely through the many difficult misunderstood phases in his development which at present often land him, through ignorance, in a lunatic asylum.

Before we conclude this rapid introduction to the subject of the Rays it is necessary to point out two more things, the first having to do with number, the second with colour.

We have said that the actual number on which the *present* physical incarnation of our solar system and our constellation was built is seven. We have been given seven qualities of divine consciousness to which to attain. But seven is not the ultimate or complete number—it is only the number which produces physical manifestation. Beyond the seven there are other numbers, other qualities, perhaps other Rays and other planets, to which our consciousness or our development has as yet little relation. Other numbers and other lessons await us in the future. Although we are basically concerned at present with the Divine Seven, we yet have been given hints and indications of further numerical entities. Twelve is considered to be the perfect and complete number, with the Deity of Deities in the centre, making thirteen. This is seen in the Twelve Signs of the Zodiac and the Twelve Creative

Hierarchies. It was symbolised for us also by Christ with His
Twelve Disciples and Himself in the centre.

So let us grasp the ensoulment of numbers little by little,
realising that there are always steps ahead of us.

The second point which I wish to make has to do with
colour and polarity, and needs following carefully. Three of
the spectrum colours, red, orange and yellow, are male and
positive; three more, blue, indigo and violet, are feminine
and negative.

Every entity in creation is negative to the plane or phase
above it in vibration, and positive to the plane or phase of
manifestation below it in vibration. Our earth is negative to
the sun, but positive in a certain way to the moon. A man is
positive to all that composes his body but negative to his
soul. His soul is positive to his body but negative in its turn
to his spirit. Therefore his soul, for instance, can have two
primary colours. Seen from 'above' by the spirit it would
have a negative feminine colour, blue (this would be its
colour seen esoterically); but seen from 'below' from the
physical or mental planes the colour of the soul would be
positive and male—tinged with red or rose or flame (this
would be its colour seen exoterically). Therefore the colouring of all things is much more complex than we imagine,
depending upon the plane from which we are conducting
our observations. It will be seen, therefore, that once we are
discussing planes other than the physical the question of
colouring is better left alone for the present.

There is a further point also in this connection. Just as the
seven Rays and seven Planes are not the complete number,
so also the seven colours of the spectrum do not complete
the colour scale, although they were sufficient for this solar
incarnation. There are the twelve colours also, grouped
around the One at the centre, including therefore five more
colours with which we cannot be familiar while our consciousness is focused in the lower planes.

Also we must realise that each great Entity who is helping to form this solar system has his Triad, or major triple division into body, soul and spirit, and that while his physical existence is focused in a particular planet (as is ours in a particular human body) his soul is focused perhaps in another planet, of quite different vibrations, just as our souls are focused in another plane, the soul-plane which is in itself an Entity.

These points give vital hints as to the nature of the secret mysteries which become revealed to the disciple at successive initiations, and upon which it is idle therefore for us to speculate at present. But what we *can* do, however, with great benefit, is to bear in mind the interchangeable, interpenetrating nature of all things as they partake of the One Life, whether it be in their colour, their polarity or their appearance and function in the different planes.

6

The Hierarchy

We have seen how a universe is organised by a division of the Divine Consciousness into separate qualities or purposes, each ensouled by Divine Spirit and therefore becoming a living Entity. The first division into three, the Triangle, was repeated four times to give the twelve divisions of complete manifestation. These divisions radiate outwards from the centre of the periphery of its influence, forming the Twelve Signs of the Zodiac. The Greater Zodiac is formed around that centre which holds our solar system in its orbit. The lesser Zodiac, that with which we are better acquainted, is the repetition of the greater process. It is performed by our sun, whose radiating influence also divides itself into twelve Signs which are a reflection of the Greater Zodiac. Through this our earth and the planets move as they circle around the sun. Our earth passes round the lesser Zodiac once in a year, taking approximately one month to move through each of the twelve Signs. Our solar system takes about 25,920 years to circle round the Greater Zodiac and complete a 'solar year'. Therefore our solar system takes about 2160 years to move through each of the Signs of the Greater Zodiac. Each of these twelve great periods is called an Age. We are passing out of the Piscean Age into the Aquarian Age at present. This is the cause of many disturbances and changes.

All the Signs of the Zodiac are ensouled by their spiritual aspects or counterparts, as are the Seven Rays and the Seven

Planes. This great company of Rulers, graded from the greatest to the lesser, form the governmental Hierarchy which controls evolution. In that vast atom, the Greater Zodiac, these Hierarchies of existences are grand almost beyond our possible conception. But the whole plan is repeated in our solar system, and repeated again on a still smaller scale within the sphere of influence of the lesser atom, our earth. At this stage it is reduced to beings some of whom are nearly human in quality and form, and therefore more possible of being understood by ourselves.

The Hierarchy is composed of 'God and his angels, Cherubim and Seraphim and all the Company of Heaven'. We will now try to define these as well as we are able.

The Solar Hierarchy is composed of the Solar Logos and his triple differentiations, the Father (Will), the Son (Love-Wisdom) and the Holy Spirit (Active Intelligence). Further emanation produced the Seven Rays. All these influences sweep through the solar system, including the tiny planet Earth. Here they are transmitted and utilised by the Hierarchy-in-miniature which governs our planet.

We will now consider this Planetary Hierarchy in detail. The Solar Logos himself is reflected by his Regent upon this earth, the Lord of the World, who has been called by many names by many nations, such as the 'Ancient of Days', and the 'one Initiator'. He is also named Sanat Kumara. He is a highly evolved Being who came to this earth from another planet.

The great Sanat Kumara is in a certain sense the Disciple of the Spirit of this planet, the Planetary Logos, which latter is himself the Disciple of the Solar Logos.

The Head of the work of the First Ray of Will is called the Manu. The words Manu and Man come from the root 'Mind'. The Manu is the Lord of a Root-race, and controls its life, development and decay. We are told that there are two Manus on the earth today—the Lord Vaivasvata, Who

is the Manu of our own—the Fifth—Root-race, and the
Lord Chakshusha, who is the Manu of the Fourth Root-
race—the Atlantean. It is said that the latter dwells in inland
China awaiting the final flowering of the Chinese and
Japanese attainment.

The Head of the Second or Divine Ray of Love-Wisdom
is the Christ, known in the East as the Lord Maitreya or the
Bodhisattva. This position in the Hierarchy is that of World
Teacher, the Head of all the religions of the world, and the
Master of all the Masters. The Christ, pouring upon the
world the Divine Ray of Love-Wisdom, the power of spiritual attraction which can hold the souls of men and of all
life in brotherhood and understanding, is approaching ever
nearer to the consciousness of mankind, because that consciousness is itself becoming more and more highly sensitive
and higher in vibration, and so going to meet the Christ halfway, as it were. This great and loving Being is striving,
through his Disciples of every grade, and churches of every
denomination, to flood the human heart and consciousness
with the wisdom and love of God, so that the heart and mind
of man may learn to function as one perfect whole, and so
move onwards along the Path which leads to unity.

The Head of the Third Ray of Active Intelligence is called
the Mahachohan. He is the Lord of Civilisation. He directs
and fosters all those aspects of human life by means of which
progress and self-expression take place. Under his care are
also the four minor Rays and the Masters who embody their
influence, in their four aspects of Harmony and Art, Science,
Idealism and Ceremony.

Therefore upon the three major Rays of spiritual manifestation we find the three major Departments of Hierarchical government, headed by the three great Spirits; the four
minor Rays of Attribute, or physical expression, coming
under the rule of the Third Ray. The three great spiritual
leaders have each a graded group of pupils to help them,

ranging from their immediate Disciples, downwards through the ranks of the Initiates to the levels of ordinary humanity. Each human being will eventually locate his Monad or ultimate spiritual spark upon one of the three major Rays.

The immediate Disciples of the Master of Masters, the Christ, are called Chohans. These are Masters who have passed beyond the Fifth Initiation. It is said that there are about twenty-one of these in the Hierarchy of our Planet. Helping the Manu upon the First Ray are the Masters Jupiter and Morya. The Master Jupiter is looked upon as the oldest of the Masters and has the affairs of India under his care. The Master Morya is occupied in inspiring many of the world's statesmen.

Upon the Second Ray we are told, helping the Christ, is the Master Koot Hoomi, who is engaged in vitalising many of the philosophic and philanthropic groups. Also the Master Djwal Khul, who is said to be one of the youngest of the masters. He is a great exponent of solar and planetary science, and a worker in the field of healing, using his influence in research laboratories and such organisations as the Red Cross.

Upon the Third Ray, helping the Mahachohan, is one known as the Venetian Master, and under his guidance are the Masters of the four minor Rays. The Master Serapis heads the Fourth Ray of Harmony and Art, and uses his influence with the Devas and Angels who are active in the realms of sound and colour, and who are to vitalise the coming inspirations in the worlds of music and art. The Master Hilarion heads the Fifth Ray of Concrete Mind and Science and works to inspire the unveiling of the truth behind form aspects, as is being done by the Spiritualists, and other psychics. The Sixth Ray of Idealism and Devotion is headed by the Master Jesus, that same Initiate who, we are told, lent his body for the use of the Christ in Palestine. He has ever since stimulated the life of the churches, and is preparing the thought of the world for the next coming of the World Teacher.

The Seventh Ray of Ceremonial Order or Magic is headed by the Master Rakoczi, who is the executive and manager of many of the plans of his brother Masters, particularly in the West. He is interested in the efforts produced by ritual and ceremony, by such groups as the Freemasons.

There are other Masters, some of whose names are not yet known. But already much of interest has been given out about the better-known ones, including details of their former incarnations.

The immediate Disciples of the Chohans are the Masters who have taken the Fifth Initiation. They in their turn have pupils who have taken the Fourth Initiation and are called Adepts. The pupils of the Adepts are usually those who have taken the Third Initiation and are called accepted Disciples. Of these latter there are already a large body in the world, making their influence felt in all walks of life. They have as their pupils all those who have deliberately set their feet upon the Path of Discipleship. These have taken the second Initiation and are called 'Probationers on the Path'. These latter have as their pupils the Aspirants of the world, who include all those in whom the pull of the spirit has begun to be too definite to be ignored, and who are trying to raise themselves from the level of average humanity.

The work of the Heirarchy is centralised in two Lodges. The upper Lodge includes devas, angels and higher Initiates. The lower, or Blue Lodge, includes all those who have taken the third, fourth and fifth Initiations. All these Disciples are in strict training for the power to work with the various forces of the various planes, and so help with the evolution of human, animal, devic and elemental life.

The Hierarchy stretches, therefore, in a long unbroken chain from those who share in the creative consciousness of God himself down to those humble helpers who are beginning to feel almost subconsciously the divine pull of the soul within them. The Hierarchy exists, not 'up in the clouds', but here in our midst, working behind the scenes in every continent, in every country; working either under the guise of our own friends and comrades, or as those people to whom we feel violently antagonistic—or working in etheric or invisible forms around us, or within us, telepathically inspiring our minds.

The Hierarchy has its home here on earth, secluded and sheltered from the noisy activities of man,' 'beyond the Himalayas'. This divine centre is known by the name of Shamballa, a sacred name of a sacred place to which all earnest students and followers of the Ageless Wisdom lift up their hearts and their aspirations always. It is said that eighteen million years ago the Angels or Lords of Mind came from Venus (body of the Fifth Ray of Concrete Mind) to establish this sacred city in which the Planet's Hierarchy could assemble and work, planting the seed of mind in the organisms of the planet earth and of mankind. The settling of these forces of Light at the sacred spot of Shamballa was actually the opening of a spiritual centre of the Planetary Logos. It is not necessary to say which centre this is, but I refer you to this subject as outlined in *The Finding of the Third Eye*, from which you can draw your own conclusions.

The point to try to grasp is that man functions, as we have said, as the mind of the Planetary Logos as a whole. The high illumined Initiates of mankind who constitute the upper Lodge of the Hierarchy must therefore represent for the Planetary Being those vital brain organs of spiritual contact whose activities we qualified under the name of the 'Third Eye'.

Shamballa constitutes, therefore, that vital centre in the planetary consciousness which corresponds to the seat of the higher mind, soul and spirit in man—the 'Third Eye', situated between the pineal and pituitary glands. But just as the real functions of the Third Eye take place in etheric matter of the physical plane, so is the sacred city of Shamballa built of etheric physical matter in the Himalayas. It is therefore invisible except as, and when, etheric sight is functioning. Man can only perceive the Greater Third Eye by means of his own lesser replica. But there are many disciples and Initiates moving amongst us today who could (and sometimes, among suitable comrades, *do*) testify to their own contact with and knowledge of that beloved and sacred city.

A wonderful description of the founding of Shamballa is given in the Book of Revelation, where it is called the true Jerusalem'. Once a year a great festival for all those who 'Tread the Way' is held at Shamballa. It is called the Wesak Festival, held at the time of the 'Wesak' full moon. The Hierarchy meets there, on the etheric levels of the physical plane. A ceremony is enacted and a flood of spiritual force is poured through this great Centre. Thus every year the spiritual kingdom and the human kingdom draw ever closer together in preparation for the great coming fusion. Initiation brings with it a gradual participation in and understanding of the activities of the Hierarchy, of which ordinary humanity can have no conception whatever.

We cannot leave the subject of the Hierarchy without touching upon a very important branch or aspect of evolutionary life whose members are also numbered among its ranks. I refer to the great Devas with their hosts of subsidiary lives. The vast Deva evolution runs parallel with the human evolution, yet it is not human. A great Deva is a God, but not one who has evolved from a man, as eventually do the human members of our Hierarchy. The Devic company number Gods, Angels, Archangels, and the lesser devas. They are called the greater and lesser builders.

When the Deity created our solar system he differentiated himself into the Divine Triad of Will, Wisdom and Activity or Spirit, Soul and Body. The first of these three, Spiritual

Will, re-divided again into the Seven Spirits before the Throne. The Second of the Triad, Wisdom—the Soul—re-divided into the Seven Rays, thus clothing the Seven Spirits with colour, quality and consciousness. The Third of the Triad, Activity—the Body—re-divided into the Seven Deva Lords, the Builders of Form, who built the planetary bodies and all that on them is.

The Deva Lords are comprised of and express energy—the energy of which matter is made—electricity. They each embody one of the Seven Types of Electricity, from which the graded atoms of the matter of the seven Planes is formed. They are actually, therefore, the Beings who ensoul the Seven Planes. They each contain, as man does, lesser Beings who ensoul and build the various organs and manifestations which make up the complete organism. We will now consider the lower three groups into which the Devas are divided. These are the Agnichaitans, who build the physical plane throughout the solar system; the Agnisuryans, who build the Astral Plane throughout the solar system, and the Agnishvattas, who build the Mental Plane throughout the solar system. We have not space here to study the vast array of wonderful beings great and tiny who, by means of infinite variations, go to make up the forms of the great Deva Lords, The spirits of the elements, the elementals, the hosts of beautifully coloured Devas working on the Seven Rays, the 'fairies', gnomes, sprites, salamanders and myriads of other fascinating beings have all at times been seen by human beings, and described in identical manner all over the world; the tiny elemental life who builds the form of the atom, working in conjunction with the spark of divine consciousness within that atom; just as man himself, although unconsciously, collaborates with the many grades of entities of the deva world who help to build his own body for him. All these fascinating wonders, and so many more that it is impossible even to indicate them, are waiting, already described and classified in many writings, for the seeker who has stretched and vivified his brain-cells to the point where he is capable of considering their existence as possible at all.

The whole Devic world is busy building the forms with the specific material drawn towards the soul by its own karmic radiations. The Builders must do the best they can with whatever substance the Ego has achieved the power to attract to itself.

The Masters have learnt to work consciously and creatively with the Devas upon the various Planes. This has been largely brought about through a growing understanding of the hidden influence and power of sound, colour and number.

It must always be remembered that the Ageless Wisdom teaches that the universal soul-life which pulsates throughout all the atmosphere is very eager and ready to ensoul and *entify* (cause to become a separate entity) any manifestation on planes lower than its own which has tended to individualise itself. Such a thing as an oft-repeated and persistent thought which has begun to take on a form of its own in the ether is easily ensouled by a fraction of that sea of life which is so eager to develop through some kind of physical or even astral incarnation. Therefore every possible aspect of life is more likely to be entified than not. This process of universal entification (the fact that every expression of existence veils a living entity) has been given a special name. This means that all things are organic, or a part of some organism, and that therefore there is actually nothing inorganic in the world at all.

Ancient peoples were aware of these things, or believed in them, as the case may be. They visualised the spirits of the elements and of all the forces in nature; they prayed to them, trying in many ways to ensure their co-operation. They tried to attract them with somewhat barbaric displays of their respective colours and sounds, and represented their qualities with dances or rhythmic movements. Much of these activities degenerated in time into automatic habits and ceremonies, as has happened also in the churches of the West. But it is most interesting to study the similarity of those early beliefs all over the world.

Throughout history there have been initiates and adepts who have worked with the forces of nature. Those of lofty and noble intent were known as White Magicians; while those who sought for power for the *self* degenerated into the Black Magicians, and were unable to manipulate any but the lower or 'dark' forces of nature.

The whole subject of magic is too vast for us to do anything but touch upon it here. The chief thing to remember is that the act of making magic really consists in understanding and working in the matter of a plane vibrationally higher than the one in which you are functioning. To be a magician while in a physical body one must be able to control, influence or create with the matter of the astral or mental planes. Each of these planes is sub-divided into seven strata which reflect the seven great Planes, so the highest, therefore, is in tune with the spiritual aspects. A Magician can work only in the stratum which corresponds and therefore responds to the quality of his own mind and aspirations.

We have now lightly sketched in a picture of our world as it is Hierarchically organised. Our next step will be to describe the process of evolution as it works out under this organisation, beginning with the long pilgrimage of man himself.

7

The Path of Initiation

W<small>E</small> will now outline the mysterious phenomenon called Initiation, as it has been explained to mankind both by ancient and modern teachers.

The Path of Initiation is the way along which all evolution travels. It is the long, slow road of development, punctuated at intervals by milestones witnessing moments when a definite expansion of consciousness, a definite step forward, was reached. These milestones are known as Initiations. They are arranged and planned in a steady sequence, which brings the consciousness gradually along to the point where it can be tuned up to vibrate at a higher rhythm. All the kingdoms of nature are moving inevitably and steadily along this well-worn Path, although in the general way so slowly that progress is difficult, from our own angle of vision, to observe. The Planetary Logos himself is moving onwards towards a further Initiation. All and every entified life within his organism is progressing at its own pace, along its own Path towards the next specific Initiation which lies ahead of it.

For the moment, however, we will concern ourselves with the progress of mankind only. For millions of years man has been reincarnating upon this earth, gradually building himself up into a well-organised, highly developed, intelligent and potent person. Finally there arrives a time when he becomes fully *self*-conscious, sensing his own powers and possibilities, from the material point of view. Ambition and egotism hold sway hereafter for many lives, until gradually the sense of higher values, and of subtler realities, the realisation of the existence of a spiritual world, creeps in. From that time average man becomes a dual personality, with a constant inner pull between spiritual and material ambition. This may be carried on outside the actual register of his brain. He may achieve gradual spiritual development, and even Initiations, without being conscious in his waking hours of that side of his nature at all. He can learn only through his mistakes and his sufferings, so it will be necessary for him to commit much 'evil' and many noble deeds in his various lives in order to develop his sense of values. Thousands upon thousands of years will pass, conditions of every kind will change. With many things to aid him, man (and of course woman) will slowly win through to his goal of human godhood—of the spiritual and the material perfectly fused, of omnipotence and creativeness on all the planes.

That is the story of the development of average man.

But there are many vital exceptions. There are certain men all over the world, living at all times in history, who have not been content to move along with the herd. They have been fired by the first glimpse of divinity which they sensed to go forward with more speed, to bend all their life and energies to the task. Some of these have been actuated by ambition, some by interest, some by devotion to the realised beauty, and some by the desire to acquire the power to aid their fellow men. They have been inspired with the 'divine discontent', and from that time forth have known no rest.

Such men are the pioneers, the vanguard, of human progress and human endeavour. They deliberately move from off the broad Path of Initiation, which is trodden by all humanity, and choose instead the narrow Way of Initiation, pressing forward to 'take the Kingdom of Heaven by violence'. By so doing they line up for Hierarchical work, and are soon observed by Those who are looking for just such helpers. Initiates are detailed off to watch and inspire and help them from the invisible planes. From all over the world the perfume of their aspirations is wafted to the Hierarchy, and rejoices the hearts of the angels.

When men have reached this stage they are called the aspirants of the world. At first they are not necessarily outwardly good people. They are often not conscious of the divine origin of their urge to go forward, but obey it blindly, spurred onwards by flashes of inspiration. If they pursue a course through several lives along one particular channel they will so develop this facet of their capacity that the Hierarchy will be able to send through them some great message, either in music, art, science or religion, for the helping of humanity. They are known then as *geniuses*. The quality of Epigenisis, or originality, has been extra-developed in them through lives of one-pointedness. To bring these divine messages through on to the physical plane successfully, these geniuses must still be strongly attached to and rooted in that plane. That is why so many of them have been quite 'Jekyll and Hyde' in character, having a mixture of characteristics at strange variance with the spiritual inspiration pouring through them. Of such a type was Wagner, whose lofty conceptions would have borne him right off the earth if he had not been safely held down by his more physical tendencies. Many other instances of this kind will come to mind.

After the pride of such achievement a genius may have to spend his next lives in complete oblivion and humbleness, to counteract the egotism so necessarily acquired, and to add quite different qualities to his sum of attainment. We do not know how many geniuses are scrubbing floors in our midst, learning the greatest achievement of all, selfless service, which Christ came to demonstrate to us. In his life he beautifully personified for us the Way of Initiation, leading to the utter sacrifice, the crucifixion of everything that is held dear in the material world, the offering of one's all to help humanity from its lowest rung, the entire abnegation of self—qualities which lie directly upon the path of all aspirants in the world.

Let us now consider a little more technically the Way of Initiation. There are seven major Initiations, which have a correspondence with the Seven Planes. At each of them the aspirant learns to function correctly in, and wield the matter of one of, these Planes, beginning with the lowest, the physical. These Initiations are taken separately by individual man, in groups by nations as a whole, and *en masse* by the great branch-races and root-races of humanity; leading in total to an Initiation in the consciousness of the Planetary Being himself.

Initiation itself is an actual change of focus of the mental vision. The development which leads up to it is perhaps imperceptible, but there suddenly arrives a moment when the aspirant has tuned up his whole being to the point where it can take on a higher vibrating rhythm. This rhythm is imposed upon his bodies by the ceremony of Initiation, performed by Members of the Hierarchy on the inner Planes. It produces in the Initiate a greater awareness, a wider viewpoint, a deeper certainty. For a moment he has glimpsed a fraction of the Plan of Creation, has touched the auras of the Great Ones, has borne the voltage of Divine vibrations. For him life is different from this moment, and although he still has free will to take the Right-Hand or the Left-Hand Path, he can never go back, he can never more remain static; he has been Divinely stimulated. From this time on things which he could not accept nor understand before become clear to him, things which he could not do before become possible to him, things which he could not believe before become facts for him. He has become anchored to the deeps within him, and is no longer at the mercy of the currents and tides of human life. Vistas open up before his inner vision, and he begins to sense the Path ahead.

He has been Divinely stimulated. But such stimulation is an impartial force, and affects both good and bad alike. The weeds spring up with the good seed. Therefore all the remaining dormant evil tendencies, all the stale thought-forms and habits, doubts and inhibitions rise up from the unplumbed depths of his nature to confound, confuse and overwhelm him. At times he feels that he is going backwards. He is ashamed and depressed to find what his nature still contains, after all his aspirations; he does not realise that this mushroom-growth will die when the sun of his spirit shines upon it more strongly, and that it is only when sediment and scum rise to the surface that they can be perceived and banished. So he struggles on, sometimes unhappy and confused while the fight between spirit and matter holds its own sway within his personality; sometimes serene and confident when the memory of his divine experience sweeps through him; ever moving onwards, against all difficulties, until by imperceptible degrees he has strengthened and developed himself to the point where the next Initiation meets him upon the Path.

The difference between an average human being and one who has deliberately set his feet upon the Path and intends to take the 'kingdom by violence' lies in the fact that, whereas average man remains the prey and the puppet of all the many disciplinary forces which are trying to push him towards his unknown goal, the aspirant has deliberately taken his life into his own hands, made himself responsible for his own progress and sought to understand and to do that which his Creator requires of him.

The average man still clings to the things of earth with all his might. He treats as a terrible enemy that being Who is doing everything to help him to learn life's lessons—Saturn, or Satan. The aspirant gradually learns to understand Saturn as the helper of the Deity, who holds under his hand the law of Karma—cause and effect—and deals out impartially and faithfully the lessons of justice and reward. He learns to make friends with this great Spirit, and to welcome each lesson of difficulty and of suffering with such eagerness (having everything in mind as only a way to reach his divine goal) that in the end difficulties become to him but fascinating challenges to his prowess. Suffering bears no more personal significance than the blows which a boxer receives while in the thick of the fight.

The difference between an aspirant and an average man is that the former has decided deliberately (albeit superconsciously perhaps) to speed up his own progress in order to help with the Plan and aid his fellow men. His challenge is at once accepted and the tempo of his life *is* speeded up in many ways. He must now pack into one or two lives the experiences and achievements which in the ordinary way would have taken him dozens of lives to work through. His accumulated Karma, which would have been played out to him at long intervals, now settles in one heap upon his shoulders. He has as much to bear as he is able to stand— but *never more*! In that way would Deity defeat its own ends.

The Initiations of individual man correspond very closely to the achievements and states of consciousness through which mankind as a whole has passed and is passing. During the rule of the Lemurian root-race mankind was learning to master the physical plane only, to develop and produce an efficient body and to synthesise and integrate all of himself which was then ready for unity—*his physical body* and its physical etheric counterpart or double. The difference between a human being and an animal in this respect lies in the fact that in an animal the etheric double stretches far outside, especially the head, and is therefore inspired from without by an animal group-spirit; whereas in a human being the etheric double and the physical body have become integrated, welded into one, so that man can be inspired and worked upon from inside—and the *individualised* human spirit can take up residence *within*. This great event, called individualisation, took place during the Lemurian epoch, affecting humanity as a *whole*. The remains of this third root-race, which still exist today, such as the Hottentots and the Australian aborigines, are ensouled by those who have not yet made any further progress, who lag behind, and are still incapable of building more advanced bodies for their incarnations. As and when they catch up they are able to incarnate next in the fourth Root-race Atlantean bodies, becoming usually the most primitive types in the yellow races; while in measure the aborigines become barren and inevitably die out.

The next Root-race, the fourth, the Atlantean, had the task of developing the *astral body* and finally of integrating it with the lower two, becoming ultimately completely under the domination of the astral (emotional and psychic) body, which became their most highly developed aspect. They were therefore extremely psychic, and given to 'magic' of certain types. Many of the early Atlanteans who have incarnated up to the present time in the Atlantean race-bodies have now moved up into the fourth Root-race, the Aryan (our own). But, having not yet taken the Aryan initiation, they still remain Atlantean in their consciousness and reactions, being entirely ruled by the emotions, excitable, superstitious and uncontrolled as yet by the mind.

The fourth great Root-race, the Aryan, whose main continent is that of Europe, has as its task the developing of the *mental body* and its integration with the lower three. When that is accomplished such people will be for a time entirely ruled by the mind. It is this development which has produced the age of science and materialism which has reached its zenith in our time. The greater part of the white race is still entirely absorbed in developing its mental bodies.

But, just as everything else overlaps, and interblends in

nature, so also does racial development. The seeds of the coming next great Root-race, the fifth, have already been sown amongst us and are flourishing on all sides.

The fifth Root-race will have as its task the developing of the *soul-body* and its integration with the lower four. This will eventually produce a humanity entirely soul-ruled, and therefore as different from the present mind-ruled one as is the scientist of the West from the Australian aborigine. The cradle of the fifth Root-race will be the American continent. Although individuals of the race can already be found amongst all white peoples, the beginnings of the racial home are already being founded in America by the mixing of races and types for the production of more highly sensitised bodies. For during the reign of the fifth Root-race racial and national divisions will disappear among all white peoples.

We can next consider the Initiations of the aspirant and their correspondence with the slower developments of humanity as a whole.

8

The Initiations of Man

THE First Initiation takes place when the aspirant has achieved complete control over the physical body, and can therefore 'wield his power' on the physical plane. This means that he can act upon the lower vibrations of that plane with the higher vibrations of his mind. For hundreds of incarnations he has been perfecting this control. His own form, the Microcosm, has repeated within itself the processes of the Macrocosm. Therefore his own life has sub-divided itself into lesser entities who ensoul the different organisms within his body. This is why, given a chance, any organ of the body will try to gain dominance and selfishly rule the rest, either by producing insistent cravings, by over-activity or by laziness; the cravings of the stomach, for instance, or the lower organs; the over activity of the solar plexus (nervousness) or of the brain; the unbalance of one gland or another; all these are manifestations of the individualism of the lesser lives, called 'elementals', which work for man, keeping his body going and therefore relieving him of infinite work himself. Whereas it is the lesser devas who actually build the organs and organism (under the direction of man's ego), it is these little elementals who inhabit, control and run them; they range all the way from the largest, who runs the body as a whole, down to the minute lives who, as we have seen, inhabit each and every atom.

These elementals are magnificent servants to man, but

dangerous masters. When under his control all goes smoothly. Their work explains the reason why man remains completely unconscious of all the intense activities, such as breathing, circulation, digestion and replenishing, which take place within him. But let him indulge and enjoy the cravings by which these elementals may seek to gain power over him, and his control of the situation will soon be lost, leading in all probability to terrible results.

When a man has arrived at the point where he is deliberately wielding full control over all the elements and elementals of his own composition, and has become Lord of his own body, and therefore in some measure of the physical plane, he enters the first Portal of Initiation. He then passes from the 'Lemurian' stage of living to the 'Atlantean' stage. Then the work before him lies in the subjugation and control of the lives and forces which make up his *astral* body. It is said that much time and many lives elapse between the taking of the first and second Initiations, because the whole of this earth's incarnation is powerfully under the influence of the astral plane. This astral plane is capable of control through the heart or heart centre. That is why the 'birth of the Christ child in the heart' is the urgent need at this stage in the development of a man.

The average man, as we know, is mostly under the sway of his emotional (astral) body. He is the slave of his feelings, which can upset his bodily functions, his mental balance and the direction in which his soul would have him go. What are these strong tides of feeling which sweep over him—likes, dislikes, passions, repulsions, loves and hates, which are usually separate from his 'better nature', and seem almost to have a life of their own? Indeed, if he once allows them to gain control over him he may be swept into committing any excess, even any crime.

The astral body of man is built up along somewhat the same lines as the physical. It is built by the astral-plane devas, and its organs and shape conform to the physical envelope. Just as the physical plane is divided into seven—solid, liquid, gaseous and four ethers—so also is the astral plane divided into seven strata of astral matter. Each stratum is graded from the lower, coarser vibrations of low passions, desires and emotions, to the higher, finer vibrations of pure, transmuted desire and love.

The initiate of the first degree (one who has passed the first Initiation) must learn deliberately to understand and control the forces of his astral body, orienting them to work and function in the higher planes of astral matter, and bringing them little by little under the domination of his will, until he is able to inhibit emotion and feeling if and when he chooses. He controls and uses his emotions, then, for inspiration and endeavour, but is *never* controlled or influenced by them.

When the Aspirant has at last achieved this control he has arrived at the Portal of the Second Initiation. He passes out of the 'Atlantean' stage of living into the 'Aryan' stage, which is the stage of the intellectual type of today. The work now to be done is the conquest in its turn of the mental body, so that the mind finally becomes an instrument completely under the control of the ego. He can ultimately direct it to think and concentrate, or not to think at all! (which is entirely impossible to most of us).

Before we go any further it is necessary to observe that development along these lines is not clear-cut and defined in its several stages, by any means. The faculty of man's free will causes much overlapping and produces a process of development which is never identical in any two human beings. It may be that backslidings, or abnormal progress, or uneven development, alters the prescribed tenor of a man's progress along the Path; but in any case many factors go to produce a complex and often baffling result. Advanced intuition and perspicacity is needed to determine the stage which some people have reached upon the Path. Herein lies the fascinating study of the psychologists of the far future.

The mental plane is also divided into seven strata of graded mental matter. The four lower strata are relegated to the Lower Concrete Mind. The three higher strata are the home of the Higher Abstract Mind. The Second-degree Initiate has to learn to gain complete control of his concrete mind, and its instrument the brain. Then he can deliberately create with his mind, either producing powerful thought-forms which wield an unseen influence (such as the thought for peace which so many earnest people are building up at this time) or bringing the thought through to active demonstration upon the physical plane, as an idea, invention or organisation. As soon as man has reached the point where his mind becomes a masterful and controlled power he has arrived at the Portal of the Third Initiation.

So long as a man is still mostly focused in the astral emotional plane his religious side is necessarily emotional, devout, fanatical—but *not* thoughtful. He wants to *believe*, but not to *know*. At his highest phase he becomes the Mystic, loving God with his heart, and feeling it to be irreverent to look upon Him with logic.

But when, after the second Initiation, he begins to awaken his mind and focus his life into the mental plane, a great change occurs. His mind turns like a torchlight upon his old beliefs, looks with the cold light of reason upon the dogmas and inconsistencies into which religious teachings have sometimes degenerated, frames a hundred pertinent questions to which no one can reply, and refuses any more to be swayed by emotional appeal into accepting any presentations. The result of this awakening—not of the brain, but of the thinking mind—may be of a revolutionary character. The aspirant may become an intelligent atheist at this time, and incline altogether to the so-called 'scientific' mode of thinking. But he is not intrinsically irreligious, for all appearances.

On the contrary, he is out for the truth, and to make that truth individually his own, through his own effort. This seeking for the truth will inevitably lead him to its Originator, through whatever channels he inquires. His mind *must* be given satisfaction. Why? Because it is his job to learn to control the mental plane, to understand and to wield in the mental world as much power as he has had at his command in the physical. The average man cannot comprehend this necessity, firstly because he does not know what real creative thinking is, and secondly because he cannot realise the practical power which such thinking embodies.

Inevitably, the second-degree Initiate shifts his interest from the heart aspect of his Creator to the mind aspect. He wants to know how things are made, and why they were made, and to what ends. He begins to sense that there is a Plan. Perhaps he chooses consciously to study these things along the lines of occultism, esotericism, or some other 'ism', which will lead him, according to his own quality, to uncover the veil which hides anywhere and everywhere the Ageless Wisdom. From then onwards his life is irradiated.

The first glimpse he has of the amazing and wonderful vistas ahead of him can, and usually does, throw him off his balance for a while. He may become 'cranky' in some way or another, a fanatic about his new discovery, trying to force its acceptance in entirely the wrong places, and to force himself into an unnatural development. All sorts of phases of development are open to him now. His course will depend entirely upon the unselfishness or otherwise of his motive. It will be his *motive*—the underlying expression of his will that primary aspect of God-hood)—which will condition and mould his life, tuning it to the key in which the song of his life will be heard, colouring it to its corresponding hue. This is why the most important factor in any individual life is the motive lying behind it. What a man does, what he achieves and what he suffers are all by-products of his motive, which should always be his principal source of concern. If the developing of his mind and brain become a sufficient motive unto itself for him at this time he will lose touch with his goal —his soul—for a period, and become a walking encyclo-paedia of theories and teachings. He will become the slave of words, unillumined and uninspired, and will dwell for a while in darkness. This will happen if he forgets that the mastery of the mental plane is but a step forwards; that immediately ahead lies the mastery of the soul-plane, and that the two can and should overlap and blend their activi-ties, because everything in life *does* overlap and interpene-trate. If he will avoid separatism in this as in everything else he will be safe.

So the Second-Degree Initiate gradually shifts his focus of attention from the Heart of God to the Mind of God; he changes from the Mystic to the Occultist; instead of *feeling* the presence of God he wishes to *know* God; to understand the workings of the Divine mind, the hidden laws of the universe and the Plan of Creation. His reaction on the threshold of this new door which is opening to him is prob-ably violent at first; for some time he may look with contempt upon the mystics, his old-time colleagues, considering them impractical, vague and even abnormal. Such psychic attri-butes and propensities as he may himself have possessed during his mystic stage, either in this particular life or in former ones, will probably temporarily disappear. Law, logic, reason and truth will be his key-words. If he follows the line of physical science he may turn his back completely for a while upon the inner 'spiritual' side of life. If, however, he becomes the student of spiritual science (the occultist) he will gradually change from one who had once possessed *involuntary* psychic gifts into one who is developing *volun-tary* psychic powers under the control of mind and will—a magician!

It is at this stage that the aspirant will probably take an

absorbing interest in the Ageless Wisdom—that is to say whatever fraction of it his Karma may allow him to uncover. Once he has discovered its existence he has found the inner anchor for his developing mental body, ensuring its opportunity for safe and true progress. Before this stage he may have accepted the Ageless Wisdom, but he will not have given it any earnest attention or appreciated its true significance, importance and value. But from now on it will gradually take first place in his life. It is at this point that a study and understanding of the Seven Rays should be of the greatest value to him, being used as a key to the understanding and analysis not only of himself and his own complexities and problems, but of all around him.

The inner spark of Spirit which informs each human being is called the Monad. The Monad clothes itself with consciousness. This consciousness forms the soul-body or Ego. Through this consciousness the Will of the Monad can begin to be stepped down into form. From the soul the will is stepped down into the abstract mind, where it takes still more definite form, as an abstract idea or inspiration or impulse. The Monad, ego and abstract Mind form the upper triad of the being called a human, corresponding to the primary spiritual Triad of the Deity: Will (spirit), Love-Wisdom (soul) and Activity (mind). The lower-plane expressions of the human being are his physical, astral and mental bodies, which together form the total of what he expresses in the physical world. This lower total is called the personality—in contradistinction to the individuality, which is the expression of the ego.

The physical, astral and mental bodies each belong to one of the Seven Rays for the length of at least one lifetime. The personality as a whole is also under one of the Rays. In a person who is as yet uncontrolled, unco-ordinated and unbalanced there is friction, conflict and pull between all these different Ray influences in the personality. A process of integration must be achieved. The physical and etheric bodies are the first to be co-ordinated and balanced together by the evolving aspirant. The next step is to balance up the power of the astral body and then that of the lower-mental body (concrete mind). Then these must all be subdued to the influence of the personality. We then have a fully integrated personality of great force, and making itself felt as an outstanding self-centred dynamic person who makes his mark upon the world.

The next step forward is for the soul to take over the control of the man's life from the personality. This latter is the sum total of inherited tendencies. It is moon-ruled, belonging to the past; whereas the ego or soul is the growing 'child of the Sun', the future soul-man or Son of God.

After the personality has been finally subdued to the soul and come under its control, we have a soul-ruled human being who views all of life from the angle of the soul. He is beginning to sense a still higher vibration within himself— that of the Monad, the spirit. The final stage of development consists in the bringing of the whole man's make-up, all of his lower bodies, including the soul, under the control and rule of his spirit. By this time his consciousness is focused in the spiritual Plane, and views and organises his life from that angle.

A man may not know, it is said, the Ray upon which his Monad dwells until after a certain Initiation. He does not even learn the Ray upon which his soul is found until he is well advanced in knowledge. But as a full knowledge of the Rays gives a great amount of data as to the characteristics, both positive and negative, good and bad, of them all, and as every living thing besides man himself is the blended expression of a certain admixture of Rays, this study gives the greatest scope for analytical delineation and determination, and for an idea as to the stages ahead for any expression of life. But it is a profound study, and one that belongs mostly to the future, because of the obvious difficulty of determining a man's Rays until human beings have developed greater sensitivity upon the subtler Planes, or become clairvoyant. Nevertheless a substantial beginning has already been made with the study and knowledge of this subject, and it is at the disposal of any who are ready to undertake it.[1]

The Third Initiation is sometimes known by the name of the Transfiguration. This is because it takes place when the concrete mind has been finally controlled and balanced up with the rest of the personality, making a perfect whole of such a vibration that the light of the soul, the fire of the inner planes, can affect it, can reflect itself upon it and can permanently illuminate it. From this time forth the Initiate is an illuminated man. He knows. He has seen for himself the inner realities and he is consciously in touch with them. He is able to recognise others of his own standard of achievement and higher; he can now understand the type of work that is being done on the inner creative planes, through the use of mind-control, sound and colour. He can begin to take his own part in doing vital constructive work on the mental plane of a kind quite unintelligible to the average intelligent man. It is therefore difficult to put this and future stages into words—in fact it is impossible. Only a few hints may be given out. It is after the Third Initiation that controlled and potent psychic faculties take their place in the Initiate's equipment. He uses these to work practically and systematically for humanity's progress.

The Initiate has now before him the next step along the Path, that of learning to live as a soul, to understand and control with his own soul the forces of the soul-plane, and to bring his whole equipment under the full control of his Monad, his divine spirit.

This vast subject of Initiation can be only briefly touched upon here. The Aspirant or the Initiate can see but a certain

[1] See *The Rays and the Initiations*, by Alice A. Bailey.

way ahead of him at all times. Each step achieved upon the Path brings to him a greater vista opening before his eyes. This applies to all those upon the Path, be they man or planet. Always there is a new great goal ahead. To all always there is the unknowable waiting ahead for them until the time when they have initiated themselves into an understanding of it.

The Fourth Initiation can finally be attained only through complete sacrifice and the uttermost suffering. The period preceding it is therefore called the Crucifixion. During it the Initiate must lose everything in life that means anything to him, and sacrifice himself even unto death. Were the beginner upon the Path to know what lies ahead of him he might recoil in dismay. But by the time he has reached the great test his soul is so strong and his character so expanded, his inner knowledge so irradiating and his sense of values so changed, that if he could count the cost ahead he would deem it but a little price to pay.

After the Fourth Initiation the Initiate can work consciously with the Devas, and co-operate intelligently and helpfully with his brethren in the Hierarchical Lodge. His knowledge of the Plan is ever enlarging, and he sees it extending beyond our solar system. His next task is to contact his own Monad and learn to be and to live as Spirit.

After the Fifth Initiation the Initiate becomes the Adept. He is now the perfect man, having mastered all the planes and all the lessons set for humanity to learn. He has passed into the spiritual kingdom, having creative power upon all the planes below. This means that he consciously creates by an act of will the body in which he wishes to manifest. This is too deep a subject for us to touch upon at this time.

The Adept or Master has now the right to choose whether he will take the two remaining Initiations, making the Seven; whether he will sacrifice himself to remain upon the earth to help with the progress of humanity; or whether he will pass onwards to realms of development outside this planet, and even outside this solar system.

If he takes the Sixth Initiation he becomes a Chohan. This gives him the power to wield the law (or work with the vibrations) governing all the phases of Planetary Life. If he takes the Seventh Initiation he may wield the law of our entire solar system.

Of course, we cannot understand what this means at our present stage of development; but it may serve to give us a hint of the glorious unfoldment which, it is taught, lies inevitably ahead of striving humanity. The Chohans, the Planetary Spirits, the Devas and the Deities, the Adepts and Initiates, are striving upwards upon the Path also; as they graduate to higher positions their places must be filled. It is from the vanguard of achieving humanity that the applicants come forth. Thus we see the tremendously important rôle which advanced humanity must play in the Cosmic scheme.

So here we have a bare outline of the process of Initiation as it has been given out to us from the Ageless Wisdom, brought up to date by present students, disciples and exponents. More and more is allowed to be given out at this time because more and more people are approaching the conquest of the mental plane, and arriving at the point where, unemotionally and steadfastly, they are gaining the right to know.

No one can take these teachings on trust. They obviously can only be proven by each person for himself. When an aspirant first begins to achieve, it is said that his 'light shines', the growing spiritual fire within him. This is perceived by those watching and waiting to help upon the inner planes. He is at once taken in charge and taught every night, while asleep, first in the Hall of Learning and later in the Hall of Wisdom. This is why it is vitally important not to squander the hours meant for sleep, but to retire early and regularly.

Finally he becomes the pupil of an Initiate, then later of a

Master. As his strength of vibration increases he is drawn into the sphere of his own group, a group of souls with whom he has worked or is to work, and who are inspired by a Master to develop upon certain lines for a definite end. He learns to become no longer self-centred, but *Group-centred*. This is a great step forward in development. From the time a man has earned the right consciously to know and to work with his Ray-Group he is no longer lonely or alone. He has tremendous support ever behind him. He knows himself to be under the eye of a Master, and to have become what is called an 'Accepted Disciple'.

9

The Psychic Centres

THE vast subject of Initiation covers, if one goes into the theory of it deeply, many of the fascinating complexities of creation. We must touch upon a few more facets of it here. So much teaching is given out about the 'Psychic Centres', called in the East the 'Chakras', that it will be well briefly to outline this aspect of the 'occult' or hidden life, as given in the Ancient Wisdom Teachings.

Every living organism, or atom, has its substance built round a nucleus and several lesser nuclei—in the atom of the chemist these are called the proton and electrons. In the human being they are called heart and glands. In the solar system we know them as the sun and the planets. In the planet itself they must exist also, but because of our relative positions they are not so easy for us to locate.

Each living atom has these principal centres manifesting on the physical plane as enumerated above. This is the outer crystallisation of that which exists in the etheric double, and is also repeated in the astral body, having also its correspondence in the mental body as well. Before a man has co-ordinated and integrated his three lower bodies all these centres are vibrating in a haphazard way, mostly at cross-purposes to each other. But as and when the bodies are controlled and steadied down to the rhythm imposed by the ego, they are finally all beating at the same tempo, and all revolving in the required direction and at the required speed.

Thus there are found in the developed disciple perfect channels or funnels running from his etheric body straight through to the inner planes. This enables electrical or spiritual force, as the case may be, to be passed successfully through to the physical plane, and gives a powerful hold on each plane as well; and this constitutes a large factor of Initiation.

The progressive development of the centres on all the planes, and in their right order, is the task before every aspirant. It is performed by him either subconsciously or consciously, as he struggles onwards life after life towards his goal. It is the perfecting of the centres which gradually changes a helpless human being into a creative god-man. Naturally the inner centres of higher vibration, those of the abstract and concrete mind-body, influence the lower ones. Their influence is stepped down to the astral body, from thence to the etheric body, and appears in the physical body as specific conditions of the endocrine glands. From this it can be seen that the mind may rule the glands, acting directly upon them from their counterparts in the mind-body, and thus controlling, stimulating or inhibiting their secretions. Thus a brain reaction of fright is flashed straight through to the adrenal glands, which, being already governed by the permanent attitude of their correspondence in the mind-body, or in the astral body, react accordingly— in one person in one way, and in another differently. In the astrally governed person fright will throw him into an ungovernable flutter; with a person who is governed by the centres of the higher mind, quiet, decisive action with just the necessary output of adrenalin will be the result.

In the human being there are seven major Centres, which were shown in a diagram in *The Finding of the Third Eye,* giving their respective endocrine glands. The human form is the Microcosm (or little replica) of the Macrocosm (the larger model, be it planet or solar system); so also is the human head the Microcosm of the Macrocosm of the human form, containing within it a replica or a correspondence to the whole body. The whole of the brain is something like an embryo, with all the organs represented. Herein lies hid a great mystery which is concealed in many symbolical writings.

In the head, which contains the chief of the *major* centres, there are also the seven centres again repeated. They are the gateways through which the mind-force of the seven Rays flows. The human being as a whole contains forty-nine centres, which correspond to the Seven Planes and their sub-division into seven sub-planes each; and the seven coloured Rays, each with their seven sub-divisions. Every one of the centres is the gateway for some specialised force which is fed through it into the human being, bringing him some necessary part of his nourishment. Each of the centres is an inlet from one of the four planes of ether. In the medium of the fourth of these, the chemical ether, the governing of assimilation and excretion is carried on. In the third, called the life ether, the forces which govern propagation and seed-producing the take effect. The second ether is called the light ether. It is the field for all activities which use the effects of light upon organism, producing the phenomenon we call colour, and building the physical senses, especially the eye. Finally there is the first ether, vibrationally the highest of them all, which is called the reflecting ether. This is a kind of subtle photographic medium, by means of which impressions can be passed from one plane to another; it is the medium through which thoughts are impressed by the mind upon the brain. It reflects all that is held by the memory of nature within the fourth stratum of the mental plane. These reflections are just like moving pictures, and can be perceived by psychometrists and involuntary or voluntary clairvoyants. Everything a person thinks, sees or has seen is reflected and stored in the matter of the fourth ether of their etheric bodies; this is where involuntary memory really exists, not within the brain; and even this is but the reflection of the true memory within the mental body. The subject of the ethers is a full and deep study, and difficult to understand so long as we have a three-dimensional type of mind.[1]

But I want to put the picture before you for this reason.

There are, as we have seen, seven Major Initiations through which pass those who deliberately dedicate themselves to tread the Path, and work to become candidates for these great expansions of consciousness and power. But, following the divine plan, these Major Seven have, as usual, each their seven subsidiary lesser initiations, making forty-nine in all. These correspond or are allocated one to each of the forty-nine sub-planes of the seven Planes of matter. These lesser initiations are gradually passed through in the ordinary course of human evolution, in any case, although it takes thousands of years longer than the times taken by the conscious aspirant. Each of these sub-planes has to be conquered by the aspirant, first within his own body by his mode of living, and secondly by his understanding, thus giving him power to act with and upon it. At each of these conquests one of his centres has been developed and co-ordinated to the point where the spiritual wisdom and force appertaining to it can gain admittance and henceforth flow through uninterruptedly. The inauguration of this flow constitutes an initiation. It is performed by those invisible guardians, helpers or Masters who have the aspirant in charge. When the aspirant has conquered or mastered all the sub-divisions of a plane he is ready to take the Major Initiation of that Plane. This involves a wonderful ceremony, which takes place on the etheric Plane at Shamballa. The candidate leaves his physical body to attend it.

Surrounded by the Members of the Hierarchy, the candidate stands before the Hierophant, the Initiator, who wields

[1] See *The Rosicrucian Cosmo-Conception.*

in his hand the Initiating Rod. This is one of the Rods of Power, through which flow stupendous spiritual forces from various of the great centres of the universe. With this Rod the Initiator touches the particular centre which the candidate has developed, thus inaugurating the flow of force through it, and linking it with its mighty higher counterpart. To the candidate is then confided the Secret connected with the Plane in question, and the Word of Power which wields the matter of that Plane, thus giving the new Initiate the equipment with which to create upon that Plane. This information is given in symbols, colours, vibratory numbers and sounds. It is up to the Initiate rightly to interpret and remember them. Herein lies the importance of a gradual mastery of the Senzar or Initiate language, acquired through a growing knowledge and interpretation of number, colour and symbol.

We are familiar with the appearance of a man, a planet, an atom or solar system upon the lowest stratum of the physical plane. But if we try to visualise their appearance as it must be when seen upon or from the upper divisions of the physical plane—the etheric strata, and upon the subtler planes themselves—we can imagine that it must be very different. In proportion as we gain etheric and astral sight a marvellous world is opened up before us, wherein we are able to see the inner workings of nature, and the wondrous forms which those workings take.

The etheric body of a man is, as we know, built from matter of the etheric plane. It is the scaffolding, so to speak, upon which the flesh, bones and tissues are moulded. It is like an infinitely fine cobweb running through all the structure. Each of its threads, like a microscopic neon wire, carries along it the Prana, or life force, from the atmosphere; the electrical rays, the solar rays, the cosmic rays; all the myriad forces which play through the four ethers and are used by the devas to build the physical form, as well as the subtler bodies. The principal channels and currents of the etheric body form the ground-plan for the nervous system, the nerve channels being in many cases built upon and around the etheric channels. Where great activity and condensed stucture in the etheric body is located we get a plexus —a close lattice-work of nerves forming a nucleus. At the heart of the nucleus we find in the etheric body a vital vortex or 'centre', which is expressed in the flesh as an endocrine gland.

When seen with etheric sight the etheric body looks like a phosphorescent cobweb sewn with stars—the centres! When seen with astral sight an entirely different appearance comes into view. The atoms of the astral are minute, crystal-shaped, scintillating and coloured, and usually in constant swirling movement. They pass outwards from the middle of the body to the periphery of the astral body, flow around it and converge inwards again—a constant rotary movement. The commencement of this rotary movement is around the centres, which appear as little revolving vortices. They revolve in different rotations and in one direction in undeveloped man; but in the Initiate they revolve in the opposite direction, very rapidly and glowing with brilliant light.

It is difficult really to describe the centres as seen from the subtler planes. It is said that in some ways they closely resemble the Lotus-flower. That is why they have been so named in the East, and why the lotus has supplied an apt and much-used symbol for them, and for spiritual development. We are told that before one of the psychic centres has become developed and vivified it resembles the closed bud of the lotus. As its powers upon the different sub-planes are born, the petals unfold one by one, and are laid open in the glory of their palpitating luminous colour. The outer petals unfold for the lower plane, the second row of petals unfolds for the higher plane, a third triplet of petals unfolds for a plane higher still. Thus the jewel within the lotus is finally revealed, the spiritual mystery and glory that lies at the heart of all.

The lotus petals vary in colouring, number and formation in the different centres. At the crown of the head is the final glory of all, the thousand-petalled lotus, the 'centre' of the spiritual body.

The psychic centres in man are linked one with another in various ways, the principal one of which is an etheric channel running from the base of the spine up into the head. At the foot of this channel sleeps the Kundalini Serpent, the fire inherent in matter. The three centres in the lower part of the body have to do with physical development and the physical plane, and form the lower Triangle. This is a reflection on the physical plane of the three centres in the middle of the body, which have to do with soul development and represent the soul Triangle. This in its turn is a reflection of the spiritual Triangle represented by the head centres.

The lowest centre is the reflection of the highest. The forces of the two must meet to produce the ultimate marriage between spirit and matter. When the call of spirit is sufficiently strong it arouses the sleeping Kundalini and draws it upwards. It progresses up the channel, vivifying the centres and awakening power and force within the disciple until the final consummation takes place. The whole subject can only be touched upon here. It is one which is better left to play its secret part, and not dabbled with or interfered with, thereby playing with fire in its most profound sense.

I will only add that the work of the aspirant is so to live in purity, one-pointedness of motive and selfless love that the correct development of the centres is achieved. This will include transferring the creative force from the centres connected with the propagative organs upwards to dwell within the throat centre, which is the centre of creativity on the mental plane. The force from the solar plexus centre, which

is of the astral desire world, must be transferred to the heart
centre, which is the centre of divine love-wisdom, where
awaits the 'Christ child'. The purified forces of body, mind
and heart finally meet in the head. Then the force of the
spirit pours downwards through the major centre and
illuminates and fuses them into one glorious whole, giving
the disciple power and vision beyond our comprehension.
This brief paragraph is all we can do to indicate this subject
here, which is too vast and complex to be more than thus
suggested.

The disciple is endeavouring to raise all the forces in his
bodies and centres to those particular centres with which he
wishes to work. These latter are all above the diaphragm.
He wishes to co-ordinate the love-wisdom of the heart centre,
the creativity of the throat centre, and the spiritual power of
the head centre, forming thus the triangle from which he can
do spiritually motivated, creative work. The ultimate aim
being creativity, it is the throat centre which gives the final
flowering of all the work.

The powers which the disciple possesses on the lower
planes are finally drawn up and focused in the centre connected with the pituitary body. The discipline of the life
finally sets up a vibration between the pituitary body and the
pineal gland which causes their powers to meet and fuse,
bringing the *Third Eye* to life between them. The pineal
gland is connected with the centre through which the Second
Ray Love-Wisdom principle flows. The major head centre,
the thousand-petalled lotus, is the one through which the
First Ray, the Will aspect of the spirit, flows. The Third Eye
is the expression of the Third Ray force, the spiritual activity
aspect. When it comes into play the will of the ego can be
interpreted and stepped down to the throat centre for
inspired activity in daily life.

The above is a very brief outline of modern up-to-date
esoteric teaching. To the newcomer it may sound perhaps

too abstract, complicated—even repelling in the demands it purports to make upon the student.

However, it is an example of much that, in various forms, has been taught in mysterious secrecy in the past history of Egyptian priestcraft and Buddhist austerities. There have always been thousands giving their lives to such studies and disciplines, because of the marvellous potentialities involved.

After all, the study of any science or art implies great effort and often sacrifice and even pain, all of which is given by the student without thought of the cost, because of the end in view. And surely the study of the science of man himself and of his Divine potentialities is vastly more important and rewarding than the lesser studies of his material achievements, many of which are only temporary makeshifts compared with that which is coming in the future.

10

Shamballa

SHAMBALLA is a sacred magic name to students and disciples of the Ageless Wisdom all over the world. Their souls yearn to it as the traveller's heart yearns for his home. To it their minds reach out in aspiration and in longing. For Shamballa is the heart of the world. And Shamballa is the mind of the world. Shamballa is the great centre in the body of this earth through which and from which the life of the Cosmic mind and the life of the Cosmic heart flows. In the same way the centres within man's brain through which a fraction of the Cosmic mind flows when they are functioning, and the centre in man's heart through which a fraction of the Cosmic Love-Wisdom flows when it is open, are both a tiny reflection of the greater manifestation of a life, which this planet is.

Shamballa, the sacred city of the seven gates, hidden in the Gobi desert, built in physical but etheric matter, remaining invisible until etheric sight is developed; in which at regular times each year councils are held by the Hierarchy, to which all those Initiates who have earned the right to work with the Hierarchy can travel in their etheric bodies, and join in the manifold branches of constuctive work for humanity and for all that lives; at which once a year, during the Wesak full moon, the great Wesak Festival is held, marking the culminating point of each year's work and achievement.

The Wesak Festival itself has been described by several of those who have been privileged not only to attend it, but to bring back a conscious memory of it. (It has also been described by many who, out of the strength of their astral desire, have built and enjoyed a little astral replica of the Wesak Festival all to themselves! But even this approach is better than none.)

The Lord of the World, Sanat Kumara, described under many names all over the world, presides over and rules the city of Shamballa, and has and will do throughout the whole of this planet's incarnation. The city of the seven gates, the stronghold of the world-mind, through which flow out the seven streams of creative force, the seven Rays—what a vital resemblance lies here with the stronghold of man's mind within his brain!—those seven psychic (or etheric) centres within his head whose consummation and flower is the Third Eye, the Lord of them all.

Meeting and working within this sacred city, using it as the mind uses the brain, and flowering from it all over the planet, are the Hierarchy. The Hierarchy are the expression, on the Second great Ray, of the Love-Wisdom of the Deity, that Wisdom which flows up from the illumined heart to irradiate the mind. 'As a man thinketh in his *heart,* so is he!' the Christ said. And the Lord of the Hierarchy, He who presides over all the spiritual wisdom developing in the heart of man, is Christ, the Master of all the Masters, the beloved Son of the Great Love-Wisdom Ray, which comes to us from out this solar system from 'THE ONE ABOUT WHOM NAUGHT MAY BE SAID'. It is the seven sub-rays of this Ray which build our solar system. That is why the God of our solar system is the God of Love.

The Ageless Wisdom teaches that when the great Christ took incarnation in Palestine He underwent a restriction, and a suffering thereby for Him, which we cannot conceive. By this supreme act of renunciation and sacrifice He took the

Initiation which brought Him into the position of the World Teacher, the Master of Masters, the Head of the Hierarchy, the Bodhisattva. This position had been held before then by that great spirit who incarnated as the Buddha, and whose work on this earth, when the Christ took his place, was finished, so that he left the earth sphere and moved away to another position in other realms.

It is said that the Buddha incarnated to embody the Wisdom-aspect of the Second Ray for humanity, and that Christ incarnated to embody the Love-aspect of the Second Ray of Love-Wisdom for humanity. Because the Christ's work came later than the Buddha's, and therefore upon a higher turn of the spiral of evolution, we can see that it embodies the most advanced teaching and ideal yet put before humanity. But it is not complete without the Wisdom-aspect. Christ Himself said : 'Be ye wise as serpents, and harmless as doves.' The latter refers to the second requisite, Divine Love. The former, it would appear, refers to what was known as the Serpent-Wisdom, the wisdom which has been in the secret keeping of humanity since the world began, but which the Buddha worked to bring out into the light of day. The serpent, symbol of this wisdom, is to be seen on the effigies of Initiate Disciples of the Buddha in the East. When through Initiation they had achieved the opening of the seven centres within the brain there is sculptured a seven-headed serpent rearing from the place of the Third Eye upon the brow.

In the East, amongst peoples who are mostly of the former great Root-race, the cry is always : 'God is Wisdom'.

To the West, for the present great Root-race, Christ brought the cry : 'God is Love'. Love means attractiveness, attraction, cohesion, synthesis, inclusiveness and understanding. It will bring about universal brotherhood, and unity and synthesis of all the sciences and arts.

Wisdom is both the cause and the result of this Love—for

the two are essentially and ultimately one.

At the Wesak Festival each year it is said that the Buddha resumes for a moment his touch with this earth, flooding it, through contact with his brother the Christ, with his great spiritual Ray of Illumination. Those at the Festival see the vast shadow of the Buddha appearing across the sky as the force pours down. This spiritual force raises the tempo of humanity (according as each unit is prepared to receive it) a step higher every year. The effect is like an Initiation in miniature of the earth itself. It brings the coming fusion with the Christ vibration in the heart of every living being steadily nearer. This fusion will finally bring about the establishing of the Kingdom of Heaven (the realm of the Fifth Initiation) in full consciousness in the minds of men upon earth. It is said that there will be another Great Appearance among men before the close of this century to further the consummation of this event; and that these factors will bring about the beginning of the Golden Age which esotericists (occultists and mystics) definitely anticipate.

The earnest prayer and desire of all conscious aspirants upon the Path is to further and help with the Great Plan as outlined in these teachings, or as they see it from their own angle of approach.

It may be well to touch here upon one other point in this teaching about the Hierarchy. That is the explanation we are given about the incarnation of the Christ in Palestine. We are told that the great Christ was a Spirit of too high a vibration to form a body of flesh. For this reason a body had to be prepared and lent for that purpose. This was done by Jesus, a high Initiate, who, during many incarnations (of which several are said to be known), brought himself to that state of perfect spiritual manhood where his body was fit to hold the terrific vibrations of the Christ. Finally he was born as Jesus of Nazareth to perform that great office. When the time came, said to be at the Baptism on Jordan, Jesus stepped out of his body and gave it over for the descent of the Christ on to this earth, Who was thus able to flood the planet with His Spirit of Love. In the Scriptures the Saviour is first called Jesus and later called Jesus Christ.

It is said that Jesus himself continued to incarnate after this, and is now permanently living upon earth as the Master Jesus. His task is to watch over and guide the developments of all the churches and inspire them to progress towards the coming religious expansion and growth.

The novelty of some of these statements comes as an uncomfortable and even unwelcome shock to many whose minds are stagnating in the moribund ruts of static orthodox doctrines. The best approach for these people is to ask themselves quite gently and quietly : 'Why should these things *not* be true?'

Such, then, is the picture which we are given of the inner strivings of human beings towards their spiritual home upon earth, the goal and inspiration of their work—shamballa.

Those who press forward towards this goal may be discovered in all parts of the world, working earnestly in some sect or group under definite tuition, or alone (as they believe), an isolated pilgrim with an inner inspiration. In the epoch which is now passing away the aspirant could best develop as a recluse, a hermit, a yogi or a monk. He gave up the things of the world, and natural human intercourse, and was able to develop spiritually only when concentrating upon that one angle of life. But now mankind has gone forward, and has gained much strength through suffering and striving, so that in this present epoch the conditions and requirements have changed. Mankind as a whole is now rapidly becoming fitted to undertake self-development and spiritual orientation, *not* any longer through a life of isolation but in the daily life of the world. Man has so far advanced in power and potentiality that he is now considered capable not only of living the spiritual life as such, but of bringing it right through into his daily living, his politics, his business and his pleasures. It is because this momentous stage has arrived that the Ageless Wisdom, hitherto so guarded and hidden, is allowed to be brought out into the open, broadcast little by little to the general public by means of books, pamphlets and societies, so that all who are ready to respond to its vibration will have the chance to do so. They will find ready at their disposal the methods of training perfected and tried out during tens of thousands of years by most of the great religious schools and communities in history. All of these advocate certain practices.[1] These include self-analysis along definite lines and the development of power on the mental plane. This can only be done through meditation. This science includes right breathing and posture, Concentration and Contemplation. Included also is the Evening Review, which helps to dissolve the Dweller[2] on the Threshold and to obviate the necessity for future purgatory. These practices are being earnestly followed by many hundreds of aspirants all over the earth. In time such an aspirant develops his own vibration and to so strong a pitch that, like a tuning-fork, he responds to and recognises his own egoic group and Master, his own place in the organisation of the Hierarchy, his own Ray and rays, and his own stage of advancement. He completes the development of the personality, becomes group-conscious instead of self-conscious, and passes from the probationer's stage into that of the aspirant's; from the aspirant's into that of the accepted Disciple; from one who hopes and believes into one who knows and does. Then the significance of Shamballa grows steadily within his consciousness (I do not necessarily

[1] See *The Finding of the Third Eye.*
[2] The 'dweller' is said to be the thought-form built by outworn thoughts and actions of the past. It is entified and bars the threshold to spiritual emancipation in its effort to preserve itself.

mean his waking brain, which is so tiny a part of the whole). He realises that he himself is now one of the conscious workers for humanity, and therefore a member on the lower rungs of the ladder of the glorious company of the Hierarchy, owning as his spiritual home and temple the sacred city of Shamballa itself.

The Initiations of the World

THE Wisdom Teaching explains that a man cannot take an Initiation until every cell in his body has been raised to a higher vibration. This involves the transmutation or casting forth of all atoms of matter of all grades below a certain rate of vibration. For a still further Initiation every cell must be raised yet a step higher in vibratory rate. Primitive man has the cells of all his seven bodies vibrating in the lowest of the seven sub-planes of each plane. For instance, his astral body would be composed of matter of the lowest or seventh stratum of the astral plane, and his mental body of atoms of mental matter of the lowest stratum in the mental plane. As he progresses through the Initiations his bodies are gradually stepped up through regular stages of transmutation, purification and exaltation, through the seven strata of each plane until they reach the top or first stratum (or sub-plane) of each plane. This top sub-plane is called the Atomic Plane in each case. All his bodies have by that time become fine, luminous, forceful channels or reflectors of the inner light of spiritual wisdom, which can then pour straight through.

In just the same way the mighty Being who inhabits a planet cannot take an Initiation until all the cells (human minds) which compose his mental body have been stepped up to a higher rate of vibration. Therefore this great Being waits upon humanity for his own advancement. The two—

humanity and the planet—are really one. When the great planetary life strives consciously for Initiation and arrives near to its portals, the stimulation he receives stirs up both good and bad throughout his whole being, influencing both devas, elementals and humans. This intense speeding-up of Karma results in a condition such as we have in the world today, where all the good in mankind and all the evil seem to rise to the surface in a rush and produce catastrophic results. Seldom in history has history been made so fast as it is being made today. Under this tremendous stimulation men in many countries gather round a leader, and an ideology. They forget themselves, they suffer, sacrifice, slay, persecute and discipline, in an effort, however mistaken and distorted, to bring about that which they feel is best at any cost.

Men are today stirred to the depths everywhere. Out of those depths are violently expurged the hidden sediment and the hidden aspirations of their natures. Through intense suffering and striving the Planetary Being, and therefore humanity as a whole, is swiftly approaching an Initiation. When humanity Initiates *as a whole* it is a very rare and momentous occurrence indeed. We are told that the last Great Initiation of humanity as a whole was at the individualisation eighteen million years ago, when animal-men passed into the human self-conscious kingdom. The coming second Great Initiation of humanity as a whole will see it pass into the spiritual kingdom (while still remaining in earthly bodies) and become spirit-conscious. This is something which can be understood only by those individual Initiates who have anticipated normal development and put themselves in the forcing-house of spiritual training as conscious Disciples for the helping of average humanity.

The Initiation to which the world is drawing very near today will affect not only all the human beings upon this Planetary body but all other units of life as well, just as the initiation of a man keys up and transmutes everything within his organism. The Devic, mineral, vegetable, animal and elemental kingdoms will all partake of the great coming Initiation, because they have themselves helped to bring it about, making it possible by their own patient progress, and through the pains of their own development. A man cannot take an initiation until he has been able to bring the organs and cells of his body under the influence of his own will-to-progress.

Then they all voluntarily co-operate with him, each and every unit of life straining to the point where it is able to take the next step upwards in vibration.

Now, what is the factor which in all these kingdoms makes initiation and progress possible? Here, indeed, is a very vital question which bears directly upon the crux of the matter, because progress continues inevitably, whether the progressing unit is objectively conscious of any part of the plan or not. What, then, is the fundamental evolutionary cause of progress, irrespective of the thinking faculty? Herein lies one of the profound secrets of nature, which it will repay us seriously to consider.

Beginning with the mineral kingdom, we find that it is already in possession of a certain state of consciousness. It can react to surroundings, be acted upon in many ways by 'chemical means', by heat and by various radiations. Some metals become 'tired', some shrink or expand. The mineral world, in fact, shows unmistakable signs of reaction—of *feeling,* of sentiency. This sentiency or feeling is still more in evidence in the vegetable kingdom. Plants and trees have been proved to react intensely to pleasure and pain,[1] they are sensitive to all the influences around them, even to the auras of human beings, to a degree which has not yet been fully ascertained. But if the subtler influences of life can so deeply affect them we can well imagine what they must endure on being eaten, cooked, cut up or burned. This is

[1] See *Experiments by Burbank.*

indeed an uncomfortable thought to warm-hearted people, but it must be faced and admitted.

With regard to the animal kingdom there is no need to point out the highly developed degree of feeling which it evidences. This is because the animals as a whole are engaged in developing their astral bodies, the seat of desire and feeling. We have only to study the advanced animals such as the dog to perceive that he is entirely focused in his astral body, which literally flings him about in paroxysms of excitement and feeling.

By the time animal-man became humanised he was able to feel definite individual pain fairly intensely. Later, when his mind and imagination have added their support, pain has become so powerful an experience that it can block out every other reaction to existence for the time being.

Now, what exactly *is* pain, this strange phenomenon which increases in potency with the upward push of evolution? What is its purpose?

In its first appearance in the mineral kingdom pain—or sentiency (feeling)—must occur, as discomfort, whenever the outer conditions of environment are those which will not allow it to remain in an unchanged condition. In this phrase lies the clue to much, if it is pondered upon. All that which pushes the mineral by slow degrees into adaptability, change, modification and finally transmutation, must be due to exterior conditions. To these impinging conditions responds the core of blazing life existing within each atom composing each mineral molecule. The whole of the universe, with its unimaginably manifold rays and forces, is converging upon the mineral kingdom. All the forces of all the planes are acting upon it, and the response is made by that great Being who ensouls the mineral kingdom, and who is the sum-total of the lesser beings within each of its atoms. That great Being knows much, and seeks initiation through those atom-cells of its body. And that great Being is itself a division, a separate ensoulment, of the consciousness of the Logos of our planet.

Initiation is achieved in the mineral kingdom, as in the human, by transmutation and radiation. This is obvious to us in the case of radium or of phosphorus. But there are many other ways in which this transmutation is taking place. Firstly the minerals in their primitive state are absorbed by the vegetable kingdom as food, blended with substances in the air, and thus transmuted or split up to a finer mineral form. Within the vegetable they pass into the bodies of animals and men, and so the process is brought to a still finer result. The higher the type of man who feeds upon them the greater is the transmutation, (provided that the food is taken raw).

There are many other factors working towards the initiation of minerals. Mining, metal-working of all kinds, contribute to the intense suffering and enduring of the mineral kingdom. Man puts it through the fires of purification again and again. In fact the present vast production of armaments must be speeding up the process considerably.

In the vegetable kingdom the same process is taking place. Trees, plants and herbs, besides being devoured, are subjected to every possible kind of treatment, by engineer, carpenter, scientist and chemist. How much they suffer in the process we cannot imagine, but it is useless, now that their extreme sentiency has been proved, to ignore the fact that they *do* suffer. Their progress and development is artificially speeded up in many cases by mankind. The transmutation and radiation in the plant kingdom is often very noticeable to us as perfume.

The intense suffering to which the animals subject each other and are themselves subjected to by human beings is the cause of bewildered despair to many a kind heart. But it all goes to build up memory and awareness, instinct and adaptability, and thereby to perfect each of the species who are still evolving. Finally the 'initiates' in the animal kingdom become so advanced that their astral bodies radiate. This radiation, which goes out to human beings as trusting adoration, can move people as nothing else in life moves them.

So throughout the kingdoms of nature pain, the great educator, steadily guards, shields, develops and instructs. Without pain all would remain inert, static. When the Initiate of a certain degree comes partly to realise the mystery and the secret of pain he grows so deeply appreciative of it that he is inclined to suffer it with joy, to welcome it—even to invite it, as some of the Eastern Fakirs and sages do. When approached from that angle it often ceases to be pain at all.

In this connection we have only to think of the extreme pain to which boxers willingly subject themselves without thinking of it as martyrdom at all; and the long-drawn-out lesser pains which such people as ballet-dancers, rowing blues, jockeys and a host of other earnest professionals willingly and unthinkingly endure. If such pain could be seen in total it would utterly daunt them, and dissuade most of them from embracing such a profession at all. If to this list we add the headaches, backaches and wrist-aches which are the lot of the mentally creative types we begin to see the tremendous amount of pain which is gone through without being considered as such at all.

Pain is therefore a relative thing; it becomes really acute when it brings to our notice the fact that we are doing something against nature which is either injuring ourselves or setting ourselves against a strong opposition of some kind. Pain is really *awareness of opposition,* just as pleasure is *awareness of collaboration,* in our environing conditions. A certain amount of opposition acts as a great stimulant to us, although too much opposition will defeat us—shock us into disintegration. A certain amount of collaboration will act as a great encouragement to us, although too much collaboration will negate our own push, and short-circuit us into the disintegration of lethargy. Therefore an exaggeration of either pain or pleasure will bring us to the same end—defeat!

Whether we are capable of feeling pain or pleasure to an extent dangerous to ourselves depends entirely on how much our lives are focused in the astral body—the instrument of feeling. As soon as a man nears the third Initiation, when he begins to live in and from the mental body, he is able to withdraw his consciousness to within the mental body, leaving for a while the astral; this means that he can inhibit pain if he so wills, and pain can no longer claim his attention to the same extent. This stage coincides with his capacity to understand the mystery and secret of pain, which I mentioned above, which he could not do until focused in the mental plane. After he has reached this stage he can look forward to the Crucifixion of the fourth Initiation without dread, because for him now both pain and loss have assumed quite other values and affect him utterly differently from hitherto.

It will be seen, therefore, to what heights and powers suffering eventually propels the advancing life-unit, whether it be in any of the four kingdoms; and how they each contribute this necessary discipline one to another. Man contributes most largely, for besides the intense suffering he inflicts he also does great and kindly service to all the kingdoms. He shapes, moulds and refines the mineral kingdom into a thousand beautiful and useful forms.

And then what happens? We saw that no sooner is a separate form produced than it is at once ensouled by a portion of the life-force seeking physical experience, which becomes an entity, and entifies the object in question. This means that every atom in that object is subjected to the following influences: (a) the life within itself, its own soul and spirit; (b) the life of the tiny elemental who cares for it; (c) the influences of the forces flowing through all the universe; (d) the influences which man brings to bear upon it through making it into a form, which are: (1) the powerful thought-forms of his own inspiration for that form, which cling to it after it is made; (2) the influence of all the people who use the object in question; and (3) the influence of the entity which ensouls it. The last three influences do much towards speeding up the development of the evolution of the mineral, changing its progress from what would have been normal progress to a forcing progress analogous to that undertaken by the conscious Initiate.

Man does the same unique service to the vegetable kingdom from a great part of which he builds intricate and beautiful forms, houses, garments, books and a thousand things which are subjected to powerful and, to them, elevating vibrations. He cultivates and develops trees, vegetables, grain and flowers to the greatest of his ability. In fact, he turns everything in nature to his use and thereby focuses his powerful vibrations into the evolving life around him, thus raising their tempo above the normal.

When, therefore, a person declares that his favourite object has its own personality, be it a statue or a motor-car in the mineral kingdom, or a wooden violin or a picture in the vegetable kingdom, he is far, far more correct than he is aware.

The developing, taming and instruction, as well as the love which man gives devotedly to the animals in large part, is easy to see. The average decent person loves animals. There were recently two broadcasts, one asking aid for ill-used children, the other for ill-used animals. The response, to many people's horror, was infinitely greater for the second than for the first appeal. This shows a feeling of *responsibility* for and realisation of the claim upon us of our brothers who are a stage behind us in evolution—the animals, in spite of our flesh-eating, vivisection, etc.

On the other hand, human selfishness does still work very

heavily against the animal kingdom. Were the public to face the facts fairly and squarely of the horrible, unthinkable cruelties inflicted upon millions of animals yearly by fur-trappers they would refuse to profit at the expense of such suffering. Unfortunately, the feeling of responsibility for the welfare of animals is only spasmodic and in its infancy.

Nevertheless, although all kingdoms contribute pain to their own members and each other's, it is man alone who contributes, as well as pain, the highest conditions for initiation to the other kingdoms of nature. He endeavours to bring animals as near to the human state as possible, which is their rightful goal. He ceaselessly serves the lower kingdoms also, towards the heightening of vibration. In so doing he gives pain, discipline and who knows how much pleasure to all these kingdoms.

The result of Pain (which is such a mysterious sacrament that I think it deserves a capital letter in this chapter) is awareness, reaction, adaptability, modification, originality, genius—Epigenisis. Note carefully this sequence. We have seen that it is epigenisis (genius, originality, free-will) which produces a spiral evolution ever moving up into higher vibrations, instead of what would otherwise become a circular groove ending in static extinction.

Epigenisis is the instrument and the builder of evolution and progress. And Epigenisis is brought into being by one agent—Pain. The will-to-be is inherent in all life. It is brought up against Pain—or sentiency—on the Astral Plane, and growth, change and progress ensue. Therefore we see that, as far as humanity and the three lower kingdoms are concerned, originality and creativeness express themselves by, through and in the Astral Plane. Here, indeed, we have one explanation of the necessity for the existence of the Astral Plane, and its place in the scheme of things.

As soon as a man takes the third Initiation and his consciousness matriculates out of the astral plane in order to live, focus and work in and from the mental plane, conditions change. He is working from above the astral plane, with higher vibrations, instead of from below or within it, with lower ones. He is working from the realm of causes, that which produces the forms. He can use or not use the astral plane at his pleasure. A large portion of it no longer exists for him, as his need for Pain has ceased also. *This is because he expresses Epigenisis deliberately, and of his own will,* and not through any pressure of outside conditions.

We now have the picture before us of the great voyage towards Initiation which is at present being undertaken by the Being whose body this planet is, and which involves every living thing upon it. We see that the extra push towards initiation in each kingdom is given by human beings, the budding Deities, who are thus already learning to express and foster divine creativeness and originality. We see the tremendous striving and struggling which is rising right to the surface at present in humanity all over the world, the willingness to suffer, to forget home and work, to throw oneself with ardour behind the ideal set up before one. Those who can perceive at this time only war, oppression, greed and cruelty, are simply seeing—what they wish to see! There is much, much more, quite easy of perception by even the average man provided he is ready to believe in the existence of good and its eventual victory, and provided he can admit the possibility of the existence of Deity's Plan for Creation. If he cannot become aware of these things it may be because he is still sunk in the fogs of the fears and thoughts of others, and cannot summon the energy to think for himself.

But it is likely that even for him this misery and depression will not last very much longer. The thought-power of those who have recognised the Plan is being added to so continuously, and is growing so rapidly in size and potency, that its influence will soon become infectious. Fifty years hence people will wonder how it was possible ever to have lived in such a befogged mentally blind state as many of us now do. By that time the first stages of the Initiation of our planet will have been reached.

Let all of us, therefore, who have become weary of 'seeing through a glass darkly' always bear in mind this picture of World Initiation, using it as a clue to the inner realities which are motivating the activities going on in the world today.

Let us try by degrees to consider the subject of Pain from a quite novel angle. This angle is not new to such people as the Chinese, and a few other races whose attitude to suffering is apt to horrify many of us who are still completely, materially and astrally focused. Pain and pressure are borne down upon this planet both exoterically and esoterically from the planet Saturn upon the Third Ray of active intelligence and *Adaptability*. The Saturnian spirit, 'Satan', let us not forget, ensouls the Third great major or Primary Ray of Deity, and wields the great Laws of cause and effect, action and reaction—Karma! That is why it is the major Ray from which spring the minor Rays, the Rays of attribute, which make up the Seven; showing that it is under pressure, pain and karma that all artistic, scientific, intellectual and civilising expression is brought to birth.

Therefore the world Initiation to which we are drawing near today is being brought to birth by a universal access of Pain and of pressure, to which humanity is responding with widespread *action,* leading, naturally, to originality—Epigenisis—and Initiation.

The World has always Known

W<small>E</small> have now sketched in further details of the Ageless Wisdom, adding a little more to the outlines with which we commenced in *The Finding of the Third Eye*. In that book it was pointed out that the Wisdom can be traced back in every continent in the world, further than history itself. Apparently it was first of all passed on by word of mouth through almost legendary and mythical priesthoods and teachers. Later it was carved, inscribed and written on ancient monuments and temples, and in a very voluminous literature, kept in the priestly archives. It was explained that the teaching was always written down in veiled language, to which there were added an outer commentary or explanation, usually very lengthy, and various inner commentaries, uncovering the mysteries still further. These were carefully guarded by the inner priesthood.

These secret writings were always rigorously hidden from the layman, because they contained teachings of how to use certain powers of nature which would be disastrously dangerous if exploited by unspiritual and unscrupulous people. We can readily believe in this connection that if the priesthood had had the monopoly and secret of bomb-making they would have kept it hidden for the same reason. The secrets which they held were just as dangerous, and just as scientific, but even more powerful, as other than material factors were involved. Whenever, in any of the ancient nations, it was desired to break the national power, an attempt was always made to steal and destroy their libraries and archives. The priesthood usually successfully anticipated this by removing their precious books to inaccessible and unknown caves and catacombs leaving only those which gave no secrets away. It is said that there are thousands upon thousands of priceless literary treasures so hidden in Tibet, China and other places, and that when humanity has developed to the point where they can be trusted with it the knowledge will reappear again into the light of day. Meanwhile, esoteric students everywhere and at all times have hunted and are hunting ceaselessly for traces, clues and fragments of the teaching. Much has already been brought to light. In this chapter I will try to point out some of the existing *fundamental* resemblances between the roots of the various religions. Remember that they were all afterwards overlaid with a wealth of distorted mythology, superstitions and misinterpretations, due to the loss of the inner commentaries and a sometimes degenerated priesthood. Gods and goddesses were transplanted to various countries when invasions took place, and suffered from faulty translation! Therefore after many thousands of years such a vast jungle of superstitions replaced the original pure teaching that it was often unrecognisable. Often the degeneration was so extreme that current religious practices constituted a social abuse instead of enlightenment.

To remedy this evil a Teacher arose at regular intervals, to enunciate once more the Divine Laws, bringing them in each instance to a more advanced stage, well ahead of the evolution of the time. In this way humanity has always had a grand goal ahead of it, even if there have been recurrent periods of the darkest ignorance.

There is a further point in regard to the sacred teaching which must ever be borne in mind. Its *innermost* form was always given in the universal sacred mystery language. This language was, and is, one which is known of and understood only by Initiates of a certain degree, although identical for those Initiates all over the world and all through history. The name of the language is Senzar. Symbols, numbers and colours play a large part in it. By the time that any Initiate has attained to a certain mastery of these he will find himself at home with and in touch with this universal secret language, and able to exchange ideas with a fellow-Initiate of any nation, either embodied or disembodied. It is this language also which is employed at the ceremonies of Initiation; therefore, the ultimate importance of an understanding of numbers, symbols, colours and sounds cannot be too deeply impressed upon any really serious student. A scrap of sacred writing, such as a portion of the Book of Revelation, sounds merely like grand poetry unless one can decipher those allusions to numbers, those poetic forms as symbols, and the meanings underlying the descriptions of colours, jewels and metals which are always given such importance. Then there are many other references found everywhere, which can be understood only after a much more prolonged study of divine science than we have as yet reached in this book. For instance, it would probably only confuse the reader to explain that our planetary astral plane is often referred to as water because it exists in what *is* water in the seven greater Cosmic Planes! This is because Deity can take physical incarnation only as far as the ethers. But these are just phrases unless they are fully explained, which is outside the scope of this book.

We have mentioned that each of the seven great Root-races is divided up into seven sub-races, which appear upon earth successively. The length of their duration, however, overlaps, so that remnants of some of them remain in existence for very long periods.

These great sub-races have each had their teacher or Prophet, who brought Wisdom to them, guided and taught them, and whose work was carried forward by his disciples and followers. The earliest races were still so clairvoyant that they recognised their teachers for what they were, and honoured them deeply. In measure, as people became more intensely material and imbedded in matter, did they fail, with the exception of a few advanced types, to recognise the wise ones amongst them. By the time Christ appeared among the mob they had become so blind and unaware that they were able to crucify Him.

The seven sub-races of the Atlanteans were as follows. Firstly came the Rmoahals, who were still spiritually attuned, and evolved the first rudiments of language; secondly, the Tlavatlis, in whom ambition and memory came to birth; thirdly, the Toltecs, who inaugurated monarchy and hereditary succession, and brought about the beginnings of nations; fourthly, the original Turanians, who brought ambition to the stage of black magic of the worst kind; fifthly, the original Semites, who were the most important of the Atlantean races, because they were the first to learn the value of the power of thought, even though they were cunning and selfish. The sixth sub-race were the Akkadians, and the seventh the Mongolians.[1] During the gradual submergence of Atlantis all of these races who survived emigration in every direction, carrying their culture with them. They set up many colonies in which this same culture, language and wisdom can still be traced. When we think of the Atlanteans and their descendants it is well to remember of how many races they were composed.

At last the time came for those to be chosen who were suited to be the seeds of the future great Aryan Root-race. This work lay in the hands of the Head of the First Ray department upon earth, the Manu Vaivasvata. He chose the people of the fifth sub-race, named by some the original Semites. He led them safely away from Atlantis and across Europe into Central Asia.

[1] See *The Rosicrucian Cosmo-Conception.*

The emigrations from Atlantis took place in successive waves over a period of thousands of years. It is said that the British Isles were then the north-eastern promontory of the Atlantic continent. Certain of the emigrants remained in Ireland and Britain and were the ancestors of the Druids. They built Stonehenge and Avebury, whose significance is only just being realised.

In this connection it is interesting to note that the forerunners of the Jews, the 'chosen race', did in all probability sojourn in Britain on their way across to Central Asia.

The Manu finally established the infant root-race upon the southern shores of the great Gobi Lake (where the desert now is). This happened about 60,000 B.C. Opposite to this settlement, upon the lake, was the Great White Island, *Shamballa,* the most sacred psychic centre upon the earth, where the Hierarchy congregated in the management of world affairs. It was thus a most significant place the Manu had chosen in which to found the new race.

A mighty civilisation was soon flourishing, which in time conquered China, Burma and even parts of Australia. Their capital was called Manova (the city of the bridge), because a bridge stretched across the lake to Shamballa. Within its glittering walls were the earliest Masonic temples. This empire reached its zenith about 45,000 B.C.[1]

Having finished his work, the Manu left the upbringing and development of the Race and its sub-races in the care of his brother, the Head of the Second Ray department, the world-teacher. This noble Spirit first incarnated into the mighty Central Asian civilisation as *Vyasa.* He was the earliest founder of spiritual Wisdom in the Aryan Race. He was to be the world-teacher during the first four sub-races of the Aryan culture. His final appearance upon earth was to be as the Gautama Buddha.

These four sub-races have developed as follows : there was

[1] See *From Sphinx to Christ,* by Schuré.

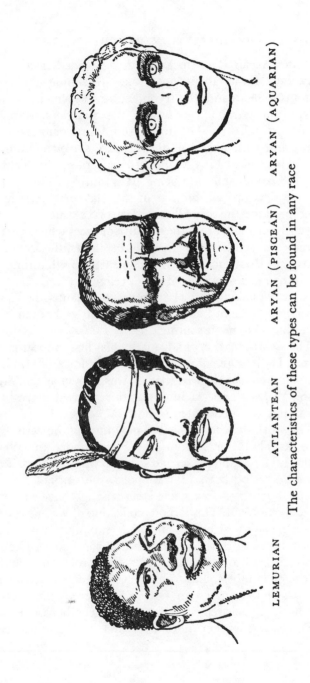

LEMURIAN   ATLANTEAN   ARYAN (PISCEAN)   ARYAN (AQUARIAN)

The characteristics of these types can be found in any race

first the Aryan Root-stock which descended from Central Asia into India about 9000 B.C., becoming the Aryan-Indians. Then came the second sub-race, which Aryanised Egypt and Arabia, giving us the Babylonian-Assyrian-Chaldean cultures. The third and fourth sub-races went south and east, giving us the Persian, Grecian, Latin and Celtic branches. Finally the fifth sub-race, the Teutonic-Anglo-Saxon, came into being. It is said that the sixth sub-race to develop will be that of the Slav peoples, who will later produce the seventh and last of the sub-races of the Aryan Root-race. From the mixture of races which are being attracted to settle in America will be chosen the seeds of the next great Root-race to come upon earth. By that time there will be no more separate nations or religions.

After the sinking of the last portion of Atlantis, the island of Poseidon, the Gobi Lake became a desert, so that the Aryans were obliged to move southwards.

The world-teacher had made his first appearance as Vyasa. He had given out the pure early form of Hinduism, arranging its teachings so that he was known as the 'divider of the Vedas'. This teaching was then carried down by the Aryan tide that penetrated India.

The world-teacher appeared next among the early Egyptians, as Thoth, or Tehuti. There he founded the Wisdom of the Light, adding a second facet to his teachings. Tehuti was said to be born in Heliopolis, the ancient Egyptian capital, about 13,000 B.C. He is supposed to have written the Book of the Dead. This famous collection of writings gives in detail the spiritual beliefs and understandings of the Egyptians relative to birth, life, death and the Plan of Creation. Tehuti is said to have also invented hieroglyphics and the science of numbers, and to have been their first astronomer. He was impersonated in Greece as Hermes-Trismegistus, and his work was repeated in the Hermetic books.

The world-teacher next appeared as Zarathushtra or

Zoroaster, the Prophet of Iran. This time he used fire as the emblem of the wisdom. Greek scholars date his life at about 6000 B.C. The story goes that an angel prophesied to his mother before his birth : 'This honoured child shall be a prophet of the just God.' Hearing of this the King Daran Sarun tried in many ways to encompass his death. But from the age of seven he was able to confound the magicians of his time, and saw through their terrifying displays. At fifteen he was acknowledged as a super-man. At thirty he withdrew to a mountain for ten years of meditation. There he was enlightened by the one God, Ahura Mazda. He wrote his 21 Nasks. He then began his mission, teaching and gaining disciples, finally living at the court of King Vishtasp of Iran as the acknowledged prophet of Iran. He gave to Iran the Zend-Avesta.

The next incarnation of the world-teacher was as Orpheus, who brought wisdom to the early Greeks. This time his emblem of wisdom was music and harmony—sound. He lived in the forests, teaching with music, playing upon his five-stringed lyre. His work was carried northwards by the fourth, the Celtic, sub-race. He was known in the north as 'Balder the Beautiful'.

It is said that he travelled to Egypt, and took shelter with the famous priests of Memphis, studying their wisdom, and receiving there the Initiate-name of Orpheus. When he returned to the languishing priesthood of Thrace they welcomed him as a Saviour. The country was overrun with the vicious worship of Bacchus. Orpheus won over the Bacchantes to the new religion, established the rule of the god Zeus over Thrace, and of the god Apollo over Delphi, finally binding the two faiths together. He laid the foundations of the tribunal of the Amphyctions, which brought social unity to Greece.

About seven thousand years later the world-teacher made his last appearance upon earth as the Buddha. This was in the first half of the sixth century B.C. This wonderful period also witnessed the lives of Lao 'Tsze, Confucius, Pythagoras and many other torch-bearers of wisdom.

The Buddha was born in northern India to King Suddho-dana and Queen Mayadevi. As the sages of that day pro-phesied great wisdom for him, the King, who had other plans, caused him to be shut away in his youth from all that might make him think. He was allowed to see only beauty and joy. After his marriage he was confronted one day, quite accidentally, with the spectacle of poverty, disease and death. This came as such a terrible shock to the young Prince that his inner nature asserted itself. He vowed to devote all his days to discover the answer to the riddle of life, and the wisdom which would bring happiness to humanity. He straightway left the court and his young wife and child. He wandered for six years seeking wisdom from all the fakirs, sages and their many systems. But in vain! Finally, in despair, he seated himself under the famous Bo-Tree and declared that he would not stir until he had penetrated to the wisdom.

In this way he finally achieved illumination, and the Initiation which gave him the right to pass away from earth incarnations to another sphere of activity. It was the first time that illumination of that degree had been reached by a human being. The Buddha then taught for forty years, giving out part of the secret wisdom. This was considered to be a betrayal of their monopolies by the priesthood. They forthwith repudiated much of what he taught. To do this they had to hide away still more of the holy writings.

The Buddha's teachings spread through China and Japan, and south to Burma. They were the consummation of all that he had taught in his former incarnations, as a study of them will show.

When the Buddha passed onwards into Nirvana, his appointed task of bringing the attainment of wisdom nearer to humanity being finished, he handed over the reins of office of world-teacher to his successor. This one was the greatest spirit as yet to contact the earth. He is known in the East as the Lord Maitreya and in the West as the Christ.

The coming of the Christ to this earth constitutes the greatest of all the Mysteries. We will not attempt to say much about it in this little book. The descent of the human spirit into matter, the human involution, had passed the lowest point in the arc, and the return of the Prodigal was about to begin. Humanity as a whole had taken the plunge into the blinding depths of materialism. It had forgotten its former inner touch with the divine world in its struggles to obtain mastery over the physical world—its appointed task. Of course, the wisdom was never allowed to die out completely, or man would have become bestial. The torch of light was ever kept burning by the few, the vanguard of humanity. As the tides and cycles of evolution rose, fell and swept by, humanity approached at periods to the joy of revelation and inspiration, or sank down into perverted ignorance, so that the wisdom had to be withdrawn and hidden from them for a while. The longest period of this ignorance was called by the Indian prophets the Kali Yuga (the black age). We are only passing out of it now. Ages and periods always overlap in their manifestations. That is why the Buddha and the Christ were able to perform their great work well ahead of time. They planted the seeds of wisdom and of love in the hearts of humanity, so that they could germinate, and so be ready for flowering when the new age is ushered in.

It has been foretold by many that this will take place before the end of the present century.

The Buddha was the most advanced of all *human beings*. He was the first one to attain to full illumination, as the crowning point of many wonderful existences upon this earth, as a teaching Initiate. Before the uncomprehending eyes of humanity he took the higher Initiations, in India, in Persia, in Egypt, in Greece ! For even the greatest Master is striving ever to higher achievement. Finally, he by his own example showed what each human being is capable of attaining. By becoming the Buddha he proved what man can do.

The advent of the Christ, however, was something quite different. For the Christ was never a human being while this solar system was in existence. He was not only the second aspect or central heart-spirit of our solar Deity Himself, but He came through on the great Major Second Ray which differentiated into this solar system. Therefore he came from outside this system. He came as the heart of Deity from the heart of the greater Deity who conceived it—but herein lies a mystery too profound.

The glorious Spirit of the Christ towered above the rest of earth's Hierarchy when he took over control of the Second Ray and became World-Teacher.

When a person is in his deepest trouble he needs the strongest help. This was the case with humanity, struggling bravely and blindly in the depths of matter, and just ready to turn inwards once more. This was why such a tremendous stimulation as that given by the Christ was needed to help the human spirit to lift itself out of matter again once its task was accomplished. This was why the Christ Spirit had to descend right into the earth and take up His abode within the subtle bodies of the planet and therefore of all humanity. He lived henceforth within their hearts, stimulating them with love and patience until they reach the time when they recognise that which is within them, and fuse their consciousness completely with the divine world, the fifth kingdom upon earth, the spiritual kingdom.

Only to those who meditate in purity of motive will these mysteries be made clear, for then the inadequacy of words will no longer be a hindrance. They will then see how the Great Ones prove in their lives to self-centred human beings that the ultimate joy and achievement lies always in service and in sacrifice, and in utter forgetfulness of the self.

13

The Birth of National Genius

For many ages before the Christ was due to take up His position as the World-Teacher He had been sowing the seeds for His future work, by 'overshadowing' certain Initiates who appeared among humanity at regular intervals. The greatest of these was known as Shri Krishna. He came to establish the wonderful culture of India as well as to lay its national foundations.

When the vanguard of the Aryan race finally descended from the Gobi Desert into India they found it already inhabited by black and yellow peoples of many grades. The powerful white Aryans conquered them without difficulty. They soon trained them in their newer arts of weaving and steel-working, and brought to them also their own religion. But the coloured peoples were retrograde compared with the new root-race. In spite of their many fine qualities the taint of corruption, of fierce animal passions and of superstition was there. Inter-breeding had been going on between the earliest black inhabitants, descendants of Lemurians, and the later yellow peoples, descendants of Atlanteans. These mixtures had produced a dangerous confusion of peoples, in whom were potentialities of all kinds. When they began to inter-breed also with the newly arrived Aryans the leaders of the latter race were faced with an urgent problem.

These leaders were the Brahmans, descendants of the early Rishis. They had been a separate and sacred class of wise men from the earliest Vedic times, and had founded the Brahman caste. They worshipped the God Agni, the fire which is in all things. The 'Laws of Manu' state that the Brahmans 'sprang from the head of Brahma', Brahma being the first person of the one God. So Brahma was the one eternal God, worshipped earnestly by the noble and ascetic Aryan priests and their followers.

Very different was the religion of the fanatical, superstitious, astrally-focused coloured peoples. They worshipped the god Siva whom they had degenerated into a terrible tyrant, who thrived upon lust, blood and cruelty. So strong and prolific were the coloured races of India that they threatened to smother the new growing Aryan population, and supplant the reign of Brahma with that of the dreadful Siva. The white Aryans began to succumb to the fascination which the coloured race often exercises upon the whites, and to intermarry with the conquered people.

The new white race was in grave danger.

It was then that the great and brilliant reformer, Shri Krishna, appeared among the troubled Indian populace, and brought salvation to it. With a wonderful insight into the complex psychology of India he remodelled the diverse existing religions into one coherent whole, whose parts were each suited to a particular section of the people. He proclaimed the existence of Vishnu, the son of the severe and ascetic god Brahma, and his messenger and mediator between earth and heaven. Thus he prepared the way for an understanding of the Christ. He then elevated Siva, showing him to be the god of nature and the elements, the shadow and counterpart of Brahma in the lower kingdoms, who through the law of reincarnation was gradually raising up the whole evolution of life towards its heavenly goal.

The Brahmans had been forced to tackle the racial difficulties in India by introducing the caste system. They established four rigid divisions of the people. The first and highest was their own, the people of pure Aryan blood, who were the directors of science and religion. Next to them came the Ksatriyas, the kings and nobles and warriors, whose blood was slightly mixed. Thirdly came the merchants and farmers, in whom the Atlantean strain predominated, showing brown and yellow skins. And fourthly came the 'untouchables'. They performed menial labour, and consisted of the lowest of the native people, in whom was found the Lemurian strain showing black skins. Inter-marriage between castes was a heinous crime.

Shri Krishna built his beautiful religion, his presentation of the great truths, to suit these castes. The Trinity of God—Brahma, Vishnu and Siva, representing Spirit, Soul and Body—were allocated very easily. The Brahmans continued with their worship of Brahma, the austere. The kings and warriors took Vishnu, the inspirer of heart and mind. The more primitive peoples kept Siva in his ennobled state. It was taught that through a virtuous life all had equal chance of reincarnating into a higher caste.

In order to raise further the moral standards, Krishna introduced the divine feminine principle to his people. He uplifted and hallowed womanhood, glorifying motherhood and love. He gave to each of the gods a holy spouse, a feminine counterpart. Thus the latent poetic and sensitive nature of India was easily aroused. Readily was woman placed upon a pedestal, and has since inspired the finest aspects of Indian life and culture.

Krishna gave to India the classic Bhagavad-Gita. He was recognised by the priesthood as an expression of the Spirit of the Rishi Maitreya, known as the future world-teacher by the Buddhists, and the Christ by the Christians. When this great Spirit appears among men once again, three powerful religions will each recognise that it is the one Saviour who has manifested to all of them. In that way will the world-religion come about quite naturally and inevitably.

There is not adequate space to make mention of the many wonderful souls, of various degrees of Initiation, who acted as torch-bearers of the wisdom throughout history. They can easily be recognised by those who are beginning to gain in knowledge and intuition.

The most important of these for us to consider was Pythagoras. This is because that great Grecian Initiate is said to be he who has been through many incarnations preparing to take over the position of the future world-teacher, after the Christ has completed His work and His fusion with humanity. Apparently Pythagoras has told us much himself about his preparation in former lives, as he was able to remember them.

Pythagoras' father was Mnesarchos, who lived upon the Island of Samos. He was a fine engraver of jewels, and some of his work is still in existence. In 592 B.C. Pythagoras was born. He was brought up in the brilliant and intellectual court of Polykrates, and thus had intercourse with many learned men. He soon proved to be the most advanced scholar of his time, although the education of that period was not along usual lines. Pythagoras began with the study of poetry and music, playing the seven-stringed lyre and reciting Homeric poems. He next studied mathematics. Finally, he set forth upon his travels to gain more knowledge. It is said that he studied with the Brahmans of India, the Magi at Babylon, the leaders of thought among the Jews and Arabs, and even the Druids, whom he visited in the west of Brittany. But his most intensive study was in Egypt, where he remained for twenty-two years with the priesthood.

When Pythagoras was fifty he began seriously to give out his knowledge. He founded the School of Philosophy at Krotona, and taught the wisdom in its spiritual, scientific and practical forms. He believed that spiritual knowledge could be attained through a study of the higher mathematics. He called his students mathematicians. The knowledge which he gave to the West, and which we have used ever since, is too well known to describe. We have kept the outer shell of it, and lost the kernel for the time being, but it still remains ready for the seeker. He was surrounded by a wonderful collection of brilliant men, who helped him to make Grecian culture the flower of the age, a glorious blooming destined to a rapid dissolution—it was too perfect to last at that immature period.

Of course, Pythagoras had many jealous and bitter enemies, and in the end they burned his beautiful school to the ground. He left public life in his disappointment, and later retired to live on the Island of Samos, where he died in 498 B.C. It is said that his later incarnations are known, and that now he is the Master Koot Hoomi, who continues to inspire humanity with wisdom and science, and to whom Madame Blavatsky[1] owed much of her information.

It was Pythagoras who consolidated and built up the foundations of Greek culture, using as his bricks knowledge that he had gleaned from many lands and supplementing it with the ancient roots of wisdom planted in Greece by Orpheus.

In the same way it was Shri Shankaracharya who appeared in India after the passing of the Buddha, to consolidate the work he had done, and fit it into its right frame in the existing religious knowledge upon which it had been superimposed. With marvellous inspiration he restored the Hindu religion and founded its noblest philosophical school. He taught that every religion was a path to God, and that every human being of every degree could attain to the highest knowledge of truth. He established four great headquarters for Hinduism in the south of India. Becoming the acknowledged prophet and head of the faith, he promised that his spirit should 'overshadow' all his successors. Thus the

[1] Founder of the Theosophical Society and author of *The Secret Doctrine*, etc.

safe life of Hinduism was assured. His successors carried on his work nobly, following on in a direct line of succession. They were each called Shri Shankara. The present Shri Shankara is the sixty-sixth bearer of the title. He is said to be a mystic and philosopher of high rank, with the power of performing miracles of healing. In this way has the development of India been taken care of.

The influence of the Buddha was not confined to India, however, but stretched in many directions, passing into Tibet, China, Burma and Japan. While Pythagoras was consolidating the genius of Greece, and India was rallying round the new faith of the Buddha, two great teachers appeared in China to do the same work for that artistic and intellectual nation. The first of these was Confucius, the name being an adaptation of the Eastern K'ung Fu'tsze (Fu'tsze meaning 'Master'). Confucius was born in 500 B.C. during the Chow Dynasty, which at this period was a time of suffering, oppression, polygamy and unbelief. His early life was one of poverty, but he soon rose to the position of state storekeeper. He was an earnest student. He began to teach at the age of twenty-two. He built up practical foundations of law and order in China, while his contemporary, the great Lao 'Tsze, was remodelling and reinspiring the religion of the people.

We have seen how this great country was colonised in earliest times by the seventh sub-race of the Atlanteans. This last sub-race was therefore the flower of Atlantean development upon the seventh—the higher mental and spiritual—plane. This explains the noble, impersonal, philosophical and non-astral character which the Chinese have borne ever since, and also the highly inspired nature of their art. Throughout a long and troubled history they never lost their true spirit, that of peaceful spiritual certainty. It needed a people who had *not* reached that stage, one in whom 'divine discontent' and mental ambition still stirred, to form the newer Aryan race. That is why the Fifth Atlantean sub-race was chosen to that end. Somewhere about 45,000 B.C. the new Aryan Root-race penetrated into China, bringing the later wisdom to the established yellow race, and infiltrating a strain of the white skin into China as well.

In the ancient chronology of China their earliest rulers have been calculated back as far as about 80,000 B.C. But their earliest definite history commences with their first emperor, a personage of wonderful wisdom called Fuh Hi, who reigned over them between the second and fourth centuries B.C. He was said to be the first great leader and teacher of the people, giving them the wisdom in the form of symbols and diagrams. These famous diagrams formed the beginnings of the classic Chinese 'Bible', called the Yih King. The Yih, or the Wisdom, means the 'Theory of Mutable Change', and purports to explain the involution and evolution of created life. Since its earliest appearance it has been the aim of every great scholar and priest in China to elucidate and explain further these diagrams and hexagrams of the wisdom. A large commentary was compiled on it by the founders of the Cheu Dynasty in about 1144 B.C. Then it became known as the Cheu Yih. Much later, after many further additions had been made, it attained to the title of the Yih King ('King' in this case meaning 'classic').

There is, I believe, a list of about 1500 treatises which have tried further to unveil the wisdom concealed in the Yih King. Four of China's greatest thinkers have written the principal commentaries, the last one having been Confucius.

The Yih King contains a series of diagrams and symbols which purport to describe evolution and the plan of creation, together with many paragraphs explaining them. We have space here only to point out the fundamental aspects of the teaching, which are :

Tai Kih, who is the one God above all, the *Greatest Utmost,* who creates the universe by emanating from himself six powers (making the seven). This is symbolised by circles placed upon a cross (the tree of life). One of these powers is called the son, the mediator between God and man; he is the beneficent power, the love-principle (second cosmic ray). The lowest of these planes or powers is called Yih, the physical plane of mutable-change.

The physical plane is built up from the positive and negative aspects of nature, or of electricity, the male and female, called in Chinese the Yang and the Yin, symbolised respectively by white and black. The originating power performs this division into Yang and Yin, the father-mother, positive-negative principles, and so we have the primary Trinity. Each of the first two forms its own polarity and again divides into Yang and Yin; the process continues until we have sixty-four divisions, each one differing in respective polarity, all numbered. These sixty-four make up the foundations for the infinite divisions of natural manifestation. (There are said to be sixty-four members of our Hierarchy, in charge of the manifestations of nature.) Nevertheless K'ih, the etheric substance cradling all things, proves the oneness which underlies all things.

Every human being must strive to become pure so that he may become a channel for wisdom, love and power, the three great manifestations of the one God, Tai Kih.

The commentaries continue to outline a deep philosophy, in which the scientific aspect is well developed, and to put forward a noble, dignified and dispassionate way of life for the aspiring soul. In the word 'dispassionate' we find the clue to the stage of the Chinese genius. It has reached the end of the road of Meditation, becoming the contemplative, who knows unity with the soul of things, to whom outward observances and words, dogma and ritual are hardly necessary, and to whom this inner union brings the continuous childlike joy which is the sign of the mind at peace.

This Chinese achievement, the perfected facet in the crystal of human development, has played its big part in the united mentality of the planet. It has always sounded the note of steady endurance and inner wisdom, and acted as an anchor of safety to the Aryan side of the world-mind during this time of intensification and strain, which without this anchor might lose its balance altogether. This service was not performed by China alone; her elder brother, Tibet, had also a part in it, and India as well, although in a different way. India, in whom so many of the sub-races, as well as three root-races, are mingled, supplies the principal training-ground for racial reincarnation. Egos are there brought into intimate relationship with the people who represent their next step upwards on the evolutionary ladder. They learn to look up to them, and to work and hope for a reincarnation into their ranks. Promotion is therefore held out to them through soul and character development only, which is an utterly different thing from the material promotion of the Western world, or of the materially-minded.

In this way India gives her contribution to evolution. All souls who have arrived at the need of this phase are said to incarnate there.

When we turn to Japan we find a different picture again. This small, brilliant country appears to be playing a unique part in Eastern development. Judging them from our standpoint of root-race evolution, it is possible that we can make a better guess at their antecedents and the roots of their intellectual and religious genius than the many vague and contradictory theories that have been put forward. When we compare them with the Chinese we can see fundamental differences of character, in spite of the fact that they are both obviously Atlantean. The Chinese is focused in the plane of intellect to the degree that he is largely free from the thrall of the physical senses, the astral emotions, or the energetic activity of the lower mind. But the Japanese is free of neither, although the artistry and intuition of the ancient race is still with him. He therefore must belong to a sub-race which came before the seventh sub-race from which the Chinese sprang. With his mind so adaptable to the developments of the Aryan Westerners, who were the fifth sub-race, his origin must have been nearer to theirs. He shows a resemblance to them in the energetic, rapid, sometimes cunning activities of a well-developed concrete mind, and the desire and capacity to go forward with Western evolution. There, however, the resemblance stops abruptly. In every other respect, the Japanese is the true Atlantean and the true Oriental. We can even trace a quality in him which proves his roots to lie slightly behind the roots of the Chinese in time. He has remained subtly nearer to the spirit world than even they have. Like the Chinese, his spiritual knowledge and faith are too ancient and inbred for words and dogma to be necessary. Although Japan has a rich store of mythology, ritual and ceremony, the Japanese in his essential nature hardly needs it. He is born with an appreciation of the fact, which we have already discussed, that everything is living, and is imbued with its own entity, from a mountain to a river, from a tree to a blade of grass. These entities are named, and treated with respect, and their aid is constantly invoked. But, more than that, every manufactured article, every ornament or piece of stuff, has its own living entity. The needle and the piece of silk, everything which is in use, has its indwelling spirit, which is always taken into consideration. The Japanese has therefore not lost that intimate union with the one spirit of life, and the many devas composing it, which he learnt first-hand in Atlantean times, and which is found in the remnants of the earliest Atlantean as well as the Lemurian races.

Sometimes, as during wars and revolutions, the true character of a nation becomes obscured under a temporary martial or materialistic influence, lasting even up to a few hundred years. But we are now thinking in terms of racial evolution during *thousands* of years, so we must not be prejudiced by the particular phases which each nation happens to be going through at the present time.

The Japanese learnt of writing from the Chinese, from whom they also took the Buddhist faith, adapting both to their own needs. With their quick minds they seize upon anything which appeals to them and build it into the structure of their own civilisation. This structure is therefore one of many-coloured bricks, wherein ancient and modern live in harmony together, wherein Buddha, Confucius and Lao 'Tsze find favour and welcome in company with the State religion of Shinto, which is the old worship of nature spirits, the Devas and all their hosts.

In spite of much borrowing, however, the Japanese has developed his own original genius as well. This is to be found in the old Samurai warrior tradition, with its Ju-Jutsu; the symbolical and sacred planting of the garden; and specialised Japanese art, to mention only a few of it's aspects.

The Japanese rushes to meet modern developments with one outstretched hand, while with the other hand he holds fast to the most ancient of his intuitions and traditions. Herein lies his unique gift and his offering to the Plan of Creation.

One of the most intriguing of racial themes is that of the Jews. This subject could easily have a volume to itself. No one has yet made it quite clear who the Jews are, and whether they are a definite race or people held together by a cult. They permeate the world without losing their individuality. They seem to possess both good and bad characteristics in excess of other nations. Their artistic and intellectual sensibilities are keyed up to higher pitch than those of other people. They have been a source of inspiration and of jealousy to many countries.

The esotericists hint at a curious theory about the Jews. They say that the Jews belonged to a former wave of evolution *before* the birth of this planet, that although they were meant to pass on to a more advanced evolution than our own, they lagged behind because of certain vices including separativeness, and were obliged to lose their place and step back into our ranks. Here they are to learn inclusiveness through blending with us. They have not learnt it yet, as we know. Yet being intellectually of a higher 'frequency' than the Gentiles they have been singled out as the guardians and the prophets of the spiritual current which was to culminate in the coming of the Christ. It was the Jews who were chosen to give the setting for the Christian drama. To make up for their past backslidings they have had to perform hard and important work upon this planet, producing by their virtues and their vices both inspiration and stimulation to the slower-powered Gentiles. It is said that, as group by group they conquer their separative tendency, they incarnate as Gentiles, who, because of the violent antagonism which the vices nearest to one's own engender, find that the hatred and persecution of the Jews is the dearest objective of their lives. So that Jews are really being largely persecuted by former Jews!

The history of the Jews is a full and absorbing one. When the Israelites became the slaves of the Egyptians they gained access to the great wealth of spiritual knowledge and tradition which was the remnant of the original Atlantean teaching. Because of their own intellectual capacity they profited much thereby. Abraham, Jacob, Joseph and Moses all held intercourse with the Egyptian priest-kings, and became initiated into the temple learning. The wisdom of Chaldea and Babylon was also tapped by the Hebrews. Soon they possessed a rich store of learning gleaned wisely from these great powers.

This learning became divided into three parts. One was

the Book of the Law and the Prophets, used by us now as the Old Testament. The second part was the Talmud, which is the collection of outer commentaries upon it, and the third is the Kaballah, which is the inner occult interpretation of the teachings. It is unfortunate that nowadays the close connection between these three is no longer understood, at any rate by the Christians, who are therefore unable to interpret much of their own literature.

The Kaballah explains how the one God above all created the world by a series of divine emanations from Himself. First there was the divine power, Kether (called also the Ancient of Days), who sent out two sub-divisions of Himself; these were Chokmah, the male-positive force (the Chinese 'Yang'), whose physical expression is the Zodiac; and Binah, the female-negative force (the Chinese 'Yin'), the great mother, the vision of sorrow, whose physical expression is Saturn. Thus was formed the great Trinity.

Further divine emanations continued. Next came Chesed, cohesive intelligence or love, whose physical expression is Jupiter, represented in the human microcosm by the left arm. (The Chinese equivalent, the 'Son of Beneficence', is represented as the left arm of the cross of the Tree of Life.) Chesed would appear to coincide with the second ray of love-wisdom of modern theosophy.

Next came Geburah, the warrior, whose physical expression is Mars; then Tipareth, beauty, the son, whose expression is the Sun; then Netzach, occult intelligence, whose expression is Venus (from whom came the hierarchy of mind to this planet; then Hod, the glory of the form, which has now been brought through as far as the mental plane, and whose physical expression is Mercury; then Yesod, the foundation, the machinery of the Universe, where form takes astral shape, whose physical expression is the Moon (corresponding to the Seventh Ray) and finally Malkuth, the kingdom, whose God-name is Adonai (our planetary spirit), and whose physical manifestation is this earth.

It is naturally very difficult to unravel the exact identifications between the various interpretations of cosmogeny, but I think enough has here been indicated to show that such an effort would bear fruit. The above Divine emanations are arranged upon the tree of life of the Kaballah. Between them run the thirty-two ways of life, or steps to the initiations. By the time these have been traversed both ways they give us the sixty-four ways of manifestation, corresponding to the Chinese Sixty-four Hexagrams and the sixty-four members of our occult Hierarchy!

The tree of life, with the Divine emanations, the Sephiroth and the thirty-two Paths, constitutes a symbolical picturing both of the Creation and Plan of the Universe, and the stages and Initiations through which the aspirant passes as he climbs the tree of life and reaches God-hood. The tree is used as the subject and object of Meditation. It contains a wealth of marvellous information as well as the stored-up force of the attention and knowledge which has been poured into it for many ages. Rich fruits can therefore be drawn from it by the intelligent contemplative.

The Kaballah, capable of ever deeper and more subtle interpretations, is a fitting symbol of the Jewish spiritual genius. The contribution of this genius to the world mentality can best be summed up by the word 'stimulation'.

It would take many volumes to do justice to the fascinating theme of national and racial development and purpose. If we accept the fact of there being a Plan of Creation, and if we agree that this Planet is a great Being whose developing consciousness uses humanity as its organ, then we must admit to two things; firstly, that every race comes into existence to lift those egos who are ready to a slightly higher rate of vibration and a more advanced development in accordance with the Plan. Secondly, that every race must

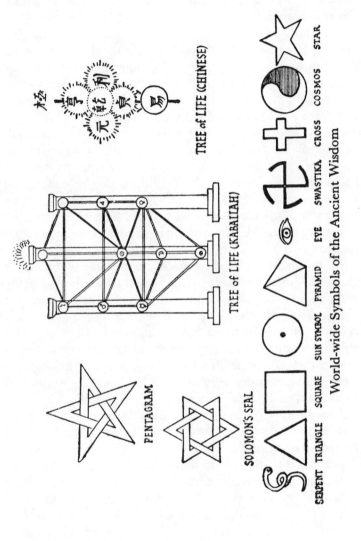

TREE of LIFE (CHINESE)

TREE of LIFE (KABALAH)

PENTAGRAM

SOLOMON'S SEAL

SERPENT TRIANGLE SQUARE SUN SYMBOL PYRAMID EYE SWASTIKA CROSS COSMOS STAR

World-wide Symbols of the Ancient Wisdom

express and give forth a certain quality or capacity which goes to complete the complex character of the Planetary Being as a whole.

We know how complex, many-sided, and ever-changing are the ingredients which go to make up the character of quite an ordinary little mortal. We must conclude that the Planetary Being has a nature at least as complex and potential, in fact, one with still deeper ramifications than a man, which we would have difficulty in comprehending. We must conclude also that the Planetary Being, having spiritual, psychic and physical 'centres' corresponding somewhat to our own, must have something which corresponds to an endocrine gland system also! With a deeper insight we might be able to locate the outermost expression of these centres and 'glands' as unseen nuclei which have attracted humanity to build many of their capital cities upon their locations.

In this light wars will be seen to be due to Planetary glandular unbalance. When one nation establishes a mighty empire for a certain period of time it might be said that during that time the Planetary Being had become 'adrenal-centred' or 'pituitary-centred' as the case might be. This will not seem too strange a statement to one who is beginning to practise in his mind the habit of seeing analogies—which, as we before mentioned, is a habit leading to inspired thinking which produces genius.

In our survey of the history of the development of national genius we have had to concentrate upon this side of the Atlantic, because the great part which the continent of America has to play lies in the future. Nevertheless, it is well to remember that the exodus from Lemuria, and later from Atlantis, spread in every direction over many thousands of years. The trek of the chosen embryonic Aryan Root-race eastwards from Atlantis across Europe under the Manu, which we have described, and which is also told to us under the symbological story of Noah and the Ark, is only actually the story of a few sub-races out of the fourteen sub-races of the Lemurians and Atlanteans. These latter provided successive civilisations all over the world, imposed and superimposed one upon the other, producing, by constantly changing conditions, the needed stimulation for the evolution of the human spirit.

Successive waves of these earliest civilisations swept over ancient America. Their progeny succeeded them as the various tribes of American Indians. The lost and buried cities of their ancestors have not yet been discovered, although enough has already been found to show their close resemblance to the early Egyptian cultures. Both the Lemurian and early Atlantean cultures have left many relics in America. The Peruvians, the Aztecs, the Toltecs—those names conceal from us marvellous ancient histories which it will one day be our privilege to uncover. Certain of the Red Indian tribes have been found to be practically identical, from a racial point of view, with the Mongolians. But without the clues offered by the Divine wisdom modern research can hardly unravel the difficult puzzles of racial heritage.

The Hierarchy reigning at the head of all human departments makes orderly arrangements by which certain of its members are allocated to care for and guide each of the root-races, sub-races and their branches. Those so instructed arrange to do this by incarnating and reincarnating in the group designated to them. By means of serving and sacrificing for this group, they take, one after another, their higher Initiations. We have touched upon some of the finest examples of this process, which can be traced throughout history and in all nations, and is even intensified at this time.

History has divided itself into two parts, B.C. and A.D. This is a natural division, because the coming of Christ upon earth marked the greatest event in its history, and one which changed the inner status and quality of the Planetary Being as well as every human item of his consciousness. Seeds must germinate in the dark. So the Christ seed implanted within the heart of humanity was able secretly to germinate during the Kali Yuga, the Black Age of outward ignorance. This, as we said, has lasted two thousand years, and is now drawing to an end. While humanity battled with blind courage and divinely driven energy towards the material conquest of the physical plane the seed safely took root, and now signs are seen on every hand of its flowering.

Throughout the Black Age—the Middle Ages, as we call them—the divine work of the incarnating teachers and torch-bearers continued uninterruptedly, albeit under much persecution because of man's temporary blindness. Their lives constitute the golden threads which have woven the real foundation and progress of human evolution; the golden history which later will be taught instead of the materialistic description of wars and intrigues which is emphasised up to date.

14

Torch-bearers of the Black Age

T HE Kali Yuga, the Black Age of Ignorance, had to come. Its advent and duration had been foretold by many ancient astrologers, as has also the coming Golden Age. These great cycles, which occur in such vast divisions of time that they are outside the average human perspective, are actually as regular and irrevocable as the lesser cycles of spring, summer, autumn and winter—and correspond to them in many ways. There comes first a period like spring, when spiritual inspiration and teaching descends upon humanity. This may last many thousand years, as it did in Atlantis. It is followed by the second period, corresponding to summer, in which humanity rises in response to this inspiration and, seizing upon a fraction of it, brings it to fruition upon earth. This gives us a long and magnificent period of culture. This period, starting upon Atlantis, was carried across Europe, as we have seen, and gave birth to the genius of various nations. The third great period is the black age of ignorance. Humanity has by then risen to the highest peak it can attain spiritually, and mastered as much of the physical world as it then may, blending the two together according to its capacity. This latter culmination was achieved in the Greek art and civilisation, after which, the peak of the wave having been reached, the evolutionary impulse sank down again to sound the depths of matter. So after the Greek illumination the age of ignorance set in. This corresponds to the autumn period when the final fruition of creative expression is given out, and the fruit drops upon the earth.

An age of ignorance is characterised by separatism and egotism. Thus we can watch the human inspiration becoming ever more contracted and personal, the mighty collective conception of the Pyramids changing through many stages until we have the finest cobweb lace created by one individual within a convent cell during the Middle Ages. Landmarks along this great change are easy to trace. We find, instead of the simple pyramid and grand plain temples, smaller cathedrals, buildings and churches, put up in greater quantities, and becoming ever more intricate in design. Great symbolic sculptures are reduced to careful portraiture, and finally to minute wood and ivory carvings. Then we see the Renaissance appear, with all its intimate, personal, emotional paintings. Poetry and literature become ever more personal and human. Music is developed, the latest expression of the divine in art. People were learning to depend more on such outward expressions of divinity than on their own link with divinity itself. The result is that their inner channel and link to divinity became gradually atrophied. That which was once truth, known and experienced and seen—became teaching. Later still it became merely superstition. Personal possessions are enthroned instead of collective wisdom.

Civilisation moved westward once more. Those branches of the Aryan sub-races who were to perform the great feat of taking the deepest, most blinding dip into matter, there to wrestle for its mastery on its own level (without the aid of spiritual insight), were being collected together in the ordained lands—France, Germany, Britain and many of their neighbours. It was now time for the lowest depths of the material world to be sounded, and, having been mastered fairly, upon its own level, to be raised and fused with the highest possible spiritual level. It will be a repetition of the Greek triumph, but on a higher turn of the evolutionary spiral. Therefore the fourth great period came, corresponding to winter, when all sinks down and hides underground, showing no outward signs of the potent and mysterious alchemy taking place beneath the earth's surface. Thus came the human winter, the Black Age, during which the seed of Christ germinated in the human heart, while man, blinded to the greatness of his endeavour, bravely copied the example so nobly portrayed for him, and plunged downwards to his own crucifixion upon the cross of matter. Thus, cut off from his divine source, even as for a little period the Christ was, he strives blindly with matter and his lower nature, passing through the crucifixion of cruelty, hatred, greed, ambition, separatism, prejudice, poverty and oppression! All these monsters of materialism, which had been suffered with resignation by those nations still keeping their spiritual link intact, were now rendered much more terrible by the greatest monster of them all—ignorance of the spirit world, and of the existence and purpose of divinity.

Such light as remained was kept burning by the churches against heavy odds. For this phase of human development attacked the Church also from its very core. It resulted in the extraordinary spectacle of the pomp and extravagance of the Church of Rome, as well as of other great religious centres. The successors to the humble disciples of Christ, whom He sent forth without even a purse in their hands, became so licentious, extravagant and over-indulged that they soon lost their divine heritage. They grew to have an envious fear of those few who still possessed spiritual knowledge, to the degree that certain of them were soon engaged in persecuting them to death, and in burning all the sacred literature upon which they could lay their hands. This phase, which heralded most loudly the appearance of the Dark Ages, can be traced in many lands. During a comparatively short period thousands upon thousands of priceless manuscripts were burnt in both the East and the West. Notwithstanding this, much that remained was hidden safely underground by the inner circle of the priesthood. We can trace this outer extermination of the wisdom everywhere. There was the famous burning of the library at Alexandria, in 48 B.C., by Julius Caesar, who destroyed 700,000 rolls; the destruction by Diocletian in A.D. 296 of the Egyptian books on alchemy and esoteric lore; the burning of all sacred documents by the Mogul Emperor, Shah Jehangir, because the Brahmans would not reveal their secrets to him; the destruction by Leo Isaurus at Constantinople of 300,000 rolls in the eighth century, and by the Mahomedans of everything they could find. We also hear of the Chinese Emperor, Tsin Shi Hwang-ti, who, wishing to be the founder of all wisdom, caused all the sacred writing which could be found to be burnt. The only one he spared, fortunately, was the Yih King, and that was because it was used for divination!

In many lands the Jewish Rabbi were the principal exponents of the wisdom and the arts and sciences. They were terribly persecuted, as we know, when this wave of anti-wisdom swept over the world. From this time onwards the wisdom had to be practised and passed on in secret and under many disguises. Its most precious treasures were completely withdrawn from all possible reach of the public and even of the outer priesthoods. All that remained for the seeker to find were the degenerated remnants of what had been magic and alchemy. These were nurtured and still further degenerated by people of the psychic peasant type. So during the Dark Ages we see the witches and sorcerers and necromancers springing up everywhere, to prey upon the superstitious and credulous in all classes of society. Without an enlightened priesthood to control them, such practices rapidly developed into Black Magic of the lowest form. From the Cesare Borgias themselves we can trace the lurid tracks of vile, obscene and murderous works performed by or under the commands of the perverted, luxurious rich, right down to the more harmless love-philtres and concoctions of the witches. The Black Mass and the Witches' Sabbath were whispered about everywhere, as were tales of vampires and werewolves. Because of the horrible forces of the lower astral plane which were evoked and entified by certain practices, many strange things were possible and came to pass. It is difficult to draw the line between what may have been fact or superstition at that sinister period.

Finally, as fear and materialism deepened, there came a time when their patrons turned upon the witches and sorcerers. A great cleaning-up took place, during which tens of thousands of them were burnt to death, the innocent perishing often in company with the guilty. From this time forth anything in the line of new knowledge, new ideas or inventions was put forth at the peril of the inventor's life. 'Sorcery!' 'Blasphemy!' cried the populace at once, and the stake awaited all pioneer spirits for many a generation. In later centuries, after many of these martyrs such as Galileo and Bruno had been proved right, men began to try to remedy the uncertainty of ignorance and materialism by laying stress upon 'science' and 'proven facts', as opposed to 'superstitions'. The criterion of a scientific fact was that it could be seen, measured, handled, or that it belonged completely to the physical plane.

In England the 'Invisible College' was formed by the first would-be scientists. The college was secret because they were in terror of Cromwell. Among their numbers were Robert Boyle, the founder of chemistry, and Sir Isaac Newton. Later, however, under Charles II, the 'Invisible College' gained royal patronage, and became 'The Royal Society'.

Thus the great schism between religion and science began. It grew ever broader, as the human character became more separative and exclusive and individual in its outlook.

Finally the Churches and the sciences each arrived at a dead end, because neither of them would admit of the reality or importance of the other's work. This latest impasse is familiar to all of us, and has brought our slight sketch of the Dark Ages up to the present day.

During this long, stormy and eventful period, which is dealt with only by our materialistic history books, the Initiates and Disciples, whose work it was to help and guide blinded humanity, moved amongst them, their light dimmed and hidden. In secret they kept the wisdom alive, enclosing it within ever thicker layers of symbol and metaphor. Secret societies, both white and black, flourished mysteriously. It was hard to know which was which. The ancient wisdom cults were never lost. Their traditions were bravely kept alive, and the torch was faithfully handed on from generation to generation.

It is exciting and absorbing to trace the Light as it filters down through history, to recognise it through the use of various symbols, signs and ceremonies; through astrological, alchemical, mystical and occult phrases which persistently occur, devoid of special meaning to all but the initiated. It is easy to enumerate some of the better known of these fraternities, such as the Knights of the Holy Grail, the Rosicrucians, the Freemasons, the Manichees, the Order of the Templars, the Alchemists and the inspired teachers who rose from time to time from the ranks of the Church herself.

How shall we begin to touch upon the rich and noble ranks of those Initiates, both greater and lesser, who followed fast upon each other, or congregated like brilliant constellations together? Their consecrated work was the fostering and guiding of these secret groups who guarded the light of knowledge, and the giving out of inspiration and wisdom to the impotent and struggling human spirit. Whom of these splendid ones, bearing the torch in all nations, shall we pick out as examples of hierarchical work upon earth? The list is long and illustrious. It is hard to know whom to choose from among its highlights.

Let us begin with the radiance of the glorious Grecian culture, where Pythagoras stood like the sun of a brilliant solar system, surrounded by his powerful lesser lights, and those who came immediately after them. Whom shall we choose amongst the great names of Greece—Plato, Socrates, Aristotle, Aeschylus? All the elements of the Greek culture, which still form the roots of our own culture today, sprang originally from their knowledge of the wisdom and the mysteries. The art of the drama itself was brought to birth during the annual festivals to the god Dionysus, whom Orpheus had introduced to his disciples as the cosmic self, the Spirit evolving within mankind. Aeschylus wrote seventy tragedies on the mythology concealing the Greek mysteries. Plutarch describes how Solon, realising the profound influence which could be exercised by the new dramatic art, caused it to be instituted as an important public cult in the city of Athens. From then on drama gradually passed out of the jurisdiction of the temples. Anyone was at liberty to write a play, and some of the finest pieces came soon to be written by men who were materialistic and sceptical in their outlook. Logic began to reign, and reason, instead of mystical symbology. While Aeschylus was revealing so much of the secrets of the mysteries in his plays that he brought his life into danger, and Sophocles was bringing into his dramas the story of Initiation, another school of thought was rapidly building up in Greece. This was headed by Socrates. It is said that in spite of his qualifications this genius refused initiation. Instead he brought to birth the worship of reason and logic, thus laying the first bricks of the foundations of the Age of Ignorance. One of his foremost followers was Euripides, in whose admirable plays the characters have become purely human, the earlier manner of stressing the mysteries of divinity beneath outward form having entirely disappeared.

Aristotle completed this work by inaugurating the method of scientific investigation of natural phenomena.

In this way the light of Greek wisdom wavered and sank before the oncoming wave of materialism. From the pioneer city of Athens the call now went out for reason and for logic ! 'Observation, analysis and reason were set up instead of contemplation, intuition and vision.'[1]

The evolutionary wave began to pass westwards. It lingered long in Italy before it diffused over the whole of Europe.

Among the wealth of interesting personalities and inspired teachers who kept the lamp of wisdom fed during the succeeding centuries one feels impelled to single out Leonardo da Vinci, the Italian painter, because his life is rather typical of an Initiate. He studied alchemy, magic, the engineering of the future, and he flowered forth in his art the subtle signs of esoteric inspiration. His all-round and inclusive approach to life betrayed him as an advanced soul.

The fourteenth century saw the work of Mani established. He was the pupil of a Persian Magi, and he founded the Order of the Manicheeans. By so doing he made himself a dangerous rival to the Church, because he reintroduced the teachings of reincarnation and initiation into the Christian faith, after they had been banished therefrom by the Church of Rome. Mani thus succeeded in solidifying Christian esotericism, and anticipating the future binding together of religion, occultism and science. His great work was carried into Hungary, France, all over Europe, and even into the East.

Finally the Pope and the King of France together attacked this new cult by ordering the destruction of its chief supporters, the Order of the Templars. All of them who were known of were exterminated and their writings destroyed.[2]

[1] See *From Sphinx to Christ.*
[2] See *Les Rois Maudits,* by Marcel Druon.

The next Initiate to come forward to the help of Western esotericism was the famous Christian Rosenkreuz. It was he who founded the Rosicrucian Order. This embodied the ancient teachings and strove still further to amalgamate them with the new department of science. This work was also done in the fourteenth century. It was carried forward in the sixteenth century by many other brilliant men, during which time it is said that Rosenkreuz again appeared as the famous Comte de Saint Germain. We must mention also Paracelsus, who was an alchemist, and put forward many of the budding ideas of science; Shakespeare and Bacon, the resemblance between whose astrological and symbolical references have aroused the famous controversy; Jacob Boehme, who showed how wisdom could still be acquired even by an illiterate cobbler; Thomas Aquinas, who tried to form a union between esoteric thought, scientific thought and the Church; Goethe, who seemed acquainted with every esoteric idea; Wagner, whose marvellous cosmic conceptions arouse the germ of greatness in every human listening soul; Swedenborg, who blazed out a torch of wisdom from the long-sleeping North; many of the poets, besides Byron, Shelley and Tennyson; and Hans Christian Andersen, whose descriptions of fairies and gnomes tallies so exactly with the descriptions given by clairvoyant people all over the earth. My readers can add to the list unendingly, and forgive me for omitting so many shining names.

Finally we come into the nineteenth century, during which the Black Age is drawing to a close, and the coming New Age is being anticipated. We must always bear in mind that ages, periods, planes, rays, good and evil, and other stages in evolution, overlap, so that there is never any definite dividing line, and interaction and interblending can take place.

We can now see the bringing to fruition of the results of man's deep dip into matter and materialism. The development of his scientific mind and the completion of his ego-centric individuality were in full swing. The beginnings of the shift of consciousness from the astral body to the lower mental body is very apparent during the latter half of last century. The mechanical age had set in.

Gradually science began to penetrate into the field of religion. It was obliged to do this outside the Churches, who were afraid to raise their eyes from their dogmas and rituals. So we see semi-religious-semi-scientific cults springing up everywhere. Everything had to be proven 'scientifically', even those spiritual doctrines which had been taken on faith through many centuries. Let us remark here that the very word 'faith' had gained its importance only after the Black Age had come upon us. Before that epoch the *knowledge*, however imperfect, that God was there, that the spirits of nature worked among men, and that a physical life was but a moment in a man's existence, was as inherent and natural in human beings as the act of breathing. But as man became further divorced from spirit and plunged in matter, the expressions *simple* faith and *blind* faith were held up to the mass of the people, while lengthy and abstruse metaphysical arguments leading nowhere in particular were the contribution of many of the trained mentalities of the day.

The Kali Yuga proper, the Black Age, lasted, of course, for a much longer period than the Dark Ages of our history books—in fact, although the light is fast breaking through, we are still living in the tail end of the Kali Yuga, as it overlaps the first beginnings of the Golden Age. The 'winter' period of which I spoke, and which was covered by the Piscean Age, is now giving place to the new 'spring' period, covered by the Aquarian Age, which will lead us right into the 'summer' of the coming Golden Age.

We will now close our survey of the Age of Ignorance by touching upon the life of the great torch-bearer who helped to pass the torch along, as it were, from the Dark Age to the Age of Science. He stands as a link between the two. In his life he showed how a man may attain to spirituality by starting out as a practical scientist. I refer to Emanuel Swedenborg, the great Swedish scientist and mystic. He lived from 1688 to 1772. After graduating from Uppsala University he studied under famous mathematicians and scientists, such as Sir Isaac Newton. While in England he invented a flying-machine, a submarine, fire-engine, rapid-fire gun, and other things belonging to a future age. He sketched these inventions, and also wrote fine poems, showing thus the all-round capacity of genius, in much the same way as Leonardo da Vinci had done. Later he became a great authority on mines and metallurgy, writing extensively and scientifically upon these and similar subjects. His eager mind turned to explore every side of nature. Finally he determined to uncover the secret of the human soul.

He resigned his office at the Royal College of Mines at the very height of his career, in order to devote his life to occult and mystical researches. He produced a great amount of illuminating theological literature. Towards the end of his life he developed psychic and mystic powers. He obtained wonderful divine visions, and foretold the exact day and hour of his own death. His life and works continue to be an inspiration to the Swedenborg Society on both sides of the Atlantic.

Living as he did, in the age of transition from superstition to science, and coming from the cold and steady North, where he could develop in comparative peace, Swedenborg anticipated the future interest in human psychology, in both its body and soul aspects; in the possibility of clarifying the meaning of much existing in the Bible, hitherto unexplained; and in the legitimate interest in psychic powers as latent in every spiritual man.

Although he lived so long ago he somehow seems in all of his activities to be a present-day character. If we link his life up with that of Leonardo da Vinci we shall recognise the one stream of potential thought, and spiritual, artistic and scientific creative genius, which ran throughout this period like a hidden golden current, from the South-East of Europe through to the North-West, and was thence carried across the ocean to the germinating root-race in America.

15

Torch-bearers of the Age of Science

SWEDENBORG died in London in 1772. In the middle
of the century a Viennese called Anton Mesmer was born. It
was he who was to carry on the former's work, by arousing
further interest, from the medical and scientific point of
view, in the innate powers of the human psyche. He arrived
in Paris only six years after Swedenborg's death, and created
a sensation by his remarkable demonstrations. He introduced
the subject of Animal Magnetism. He claimed it to be
capable, while flowing from the human finger-tips, of producing local or general anaesthesia, putting subjects into a
trance, during which operations could be painlessly performed. As anaesthetics were unknown at this time a tremendous interest was aroused. This interest was further
stimulated when it was found that clairvoyance and other
abnormal faculties were liable to be aroused under the
influence of mesmeric trance.

The next step in the coming sciences of the psyche was
introduced by Dr. James Braid in 1843. He instigated the
beginning of the study of hypnotism. Whereas mesmerism
was considered to be a physical process, using physical
effluvia through the medium of passes and strokings, hypnotism worked directly through the mind by using 'suggestion',
and by imposing the will upon a willing or involuntary subject. It was soon discovered that, while in hypnotic trance,
the subject could be made to project his or her mind almost

instantaneously through either space or time, and report accurately upon all that was heard or observed. The subject was also able to perform feats quite impossible to him in waking life. From this time onwards ceaseless experiments, voluminous writings and endless controversies have been carried on. These sciences have been patiently developed, and many eminent brains have given them their interest and support.

In about 1848 the modern Spiritualist movement had its inception in New York. By about 1852 the first American mediums arrived in England. The study was soon taken up in France. In 1882 the British Society for Psychical Research was established. From that time onwards the Spiritualist movement has increased to very large proportions. Throughout its many branches and its numerous 'circles' it has catered to every grade of mentality, from the most primitive personal methods of attempting to prove individual survival to the really scientific high-grade occult instructions which are given out by the more advanced type of 'guide'. Spiritualism is thus doing its big share of the work of bringing science, religion and occultism together. We may expect much of interest from that direction in the future.

While Spiritualism was looking after the development of an intelligent interest in the various strata of the astral plane another great movement was instilling into humanity a realisation of the powers of the higher mind and the will. This was Christian Science, founded by Mary Baker Eddy. Her ideas when put into practice soon reoriented the lives of her followers, who were learning the instantaneous power that mind can exert over matter when it is propelled by the will energised by faith in the power of divine spirit. While the Spiritualists were studying the results obtained through human negativity (mediumship) the Christian Scientists demonstrated the results to be attained by human positivity (faith and will). At first these groups worked in isolation from each other. But the nearer each group approaches to the truth the nearer will they inevitably approach to each other until the time when they can quite naturally link up.

During this period, the Theosophical Society was founded by Madame Helena P. Blavatsky. She drew together the nucleus of all those people who were ready to take up the study of the occult sciences in earnest once again. She gave them plenty of material to work with and wrote several astonishing books, full of a wealth of information about the Ancient Wisdom, much of which was said to be communicated to her through two of the Masters themselves. Her books, especially *The Secret Doctrine,* became the 'Bible' of the modern esoteric movements, and the source for many further additions to their literature. Her work was carried forward by Annie Besant and others of her disciples. Like many of the Initiates throughout history, Madame Blavatsky had a complex personality, calculated to turn away from her movement many who could not judge her work upon its own merits, irrespective of any personal associations. She has been called a charlatan because she sometimes gave way to an impish sense of humour—but her work remains, and speaks adequately for itself and for her.

The name *Theosophist* does not solely belong, however, to the followers of Madame Blavatsky and her society. The dictionary tells us that theosophy can mean 'any of various ancient and modern philosophies professing to attain to a knowledge of God by spiritual ecstasy, direct intuition or special individual relations'. This, we can see, covers a wide range. It might be applied to many of the enormous number of cults, sects, fraternities, groups and societies which have sprung up everywhere during this present century. Their number is now legion. It would take a regiment of secretaries to compile anything like a complete record of them. They are to be found in every land, but it is not surprising to discover that the greatest colony of them exists in America, and is centred at Los Angeles. This is still less astonishing when we remember that that particular district is said to be marked out as one of the high-powered 'centres' in the body of the planet, whose full development is yet to come.

One of the most famous theosophists was Dr. Rudolph Steiner. He founded a very virile movement, in which special attention was given to the study of music, dancing and the fine arts in their relationship to spiritual science.

The Anthroposophists also contribute very valuable work from a slightly different angle. They make a deep occultly scientific study of nature and the universe, seeking through practical experiments and tests to prove the unity and interplay of the one life throughout all.

As the time had arrived when it was permitted to bring the Ageless Wisdom little by little out into the light of day once more, such fraternities as the Rosicrucians began also to give out their teachings and doctrines. The intelligent seeker is able to see the tremendous similarity existing between the wisdom which is thus being divulged on all sides and, for instance, that given out by Madame Blavatsky and her colleagues, that shown forth by the Rosicrucians, by Rudolph Steiner, by the latest teachings through spiritualist mediums, by those in secret within Freemasonry, and by many others too numerous to mention.

The main theosophical lodges were eventually firmly established upon the teachings given out by the masters of the wisdom, through Madame Blavatsky's mediumship, in the middle of the nineteenth century. Half a century later humanity was considered to be ready to receive a further and deeper section of the teaching, to bring it right up to date. This was undertaken by the Master Djwal Khul, who telepathically dictated a series of books to Alice Bailey. These cover a wide field, from modern training for disciples; advanced study of the Cosmic Rays; international relationships and a future world religion. It is said that this will be formed when the Christ of the West reappears amongst men and is recognised to be identical with the awaited Maitreya of the Eastern Teachings.

The sum and substance of the wisdom, as it is given to us today through modern sources, can easily be identified with the sum and substance of the wisdom as it was known in its essence by all the civilisations and nations of the world, as they were formed one by one. This is understandable when we realise that it is and has always been one and the same wisdom, given out to suit the needs of each race, stage and period, by the long continuous chain of disciples working under the head of the second ray of love-wisdom—the Christ. While humanity was still youthful and adolescent the teaching was given direct by the highest Initiates manifesting upon earth. Now that humanity is fast becoming adult and independent, and many of the Initiates have reached Masterhood and Adeptship, the latter work more from the background, inspiring and teaching all leaders and groups. These include not only those of the type we have been discussing, but also many whom, because of their first-ray destructive quality, we in our ignorance consider evil. Old forms must be broken up continually to make way for the new. Humanity must be urged on by suffering and striving. There must be pioneers who are responsible for seeing that this important side of development is assured. Such a person as a dictator, whether he knows it or not, is working directly in accordance with his Rays, and fulfilling, either adequately or not, the desire and plan of Those who use him as their instrument.

If it needs perpetual threats of war, war itself, strain, anxiety and crisis to give humanity the final push over the brink of materialism into the waters of the new Age of Aquarius, then those who have vision will welcome the intense battering to which humanity is subjecting itself at present, seeing it for what it is—the very dark before the immediate dawn.

In our brief study of the pioneers of the present age we cannot omit to pay a tribute of gratitude and reverence to the Church herself. Throughout the long ages of conflict, of ignorance, of confusion, of lassitude, of scientific atheism the Church has stood firm. In whatever she may have failed she has remained steadfastly in existence, rooted deeply in the fabric of human life, continuing ever faithful, throughout all her phases of luxury, of persecution, of blindness, of bigotry, and even of ignorance of her own guarded truths. We must never forget that the Church is made up, and has always been made up, of human beings; and that these human beings have been subjected to all those stages of development through which humanity has passed as a whole. The Church is under spiritual laws as well as everything else. The Church can only give out to humanity in accordance with what humanity gives to the Church. I am not talking here of money or possessions, but of spiritual striving, of intelligence, mental activity and devotion.

It is true that the Church has lagged behind in certain ways. She has, unfortunately, because of her temporary divorce from the Ageless Wisdom, been unaware of the changes through which humanity was bound to pass during this inception of the Aquarian Age. She was unaware that the normal development of humanity would be from the astrally-focused devotional mystic attitude to the mentally-focused studious occult attitude, which latter will lead human beings intelligently to apply spiritual scientific facts and laws to everything in their everyday lives. This will lead to a perfect synthesis between man and his religion. But the Church was not prepared for this change, and did not, and perhaps still does not, understand it. It is likely that this was purposely arranged in order that man might achieve his spiritual independence and adulthood. It is likely that it will be the layman himself who, having blended life, science and religion to his own understanding, will in his turn offer the rich fruits of his independent efforts back in gratitude to the Church. And then churchman and layman will beautify and develop the Church still further to suit modern needs and coming changes.

Furthermore, it must be borne in mind that the Church —and I am here speaking of the Church of all denominations and of every land—is under the direct supervision, we are told, of the Master Jesus Himself, Who is living permanently in a physical body upon this earth, working continually with the other Masters and with His own present disciples. Therefore the remarks which one sometimes hears that 'the day of the Church is over' are deserving only of dismissal with a smile! The people who give vent to them are those who wish neither to go to church nor to help in its improvement. They are merely expressing what the psychologists would call their own 'wish-life'. Fortunately they are in a small minority, compared with those others, the new ones, who, belonging already to the Aquarian Age, are out to seek and determine their spiritual loyalties for themselves.

16

Completing the Picture

W E have now come to the end of the first part of our study, the survey of the spiritual, esoteric or occult sciences. We will round off this survey by lightly sketching in some of the many remaining angles of esoteric lore, which bring each, when honestly pursued, its contribution to the general whole.

I have already introduced the subjects of astrology, symbols and colours, the science of numbers and the practices of 'yoga' and meditation to my readers.[1] Having shown how life continually repeats and reflects its pattern and its message everywhere, we cannot afford to dismiss such a science as palmistry without consideration.

The hand is the most sensitive and highly developed link with the brain. It is the recipient of perpetual streams of messages arriving as impulses, electrical in character, from the brain. Everything that a man *is* finds expression in some way in his hands. Both the hands are also under different influences, being respectively on the positive and negative sides of the body. A short study of the rules of palmistry will soon convince the reader that here is a consideration of the universe and its forces in miniature reflection, the microcosm of man being still further reduced to the microcosm of his hand. The fact that in blind people the grey matter of the brain is sometimes found in the tips of their fingers shows how nearly allied to the brain a hand can be. It is not so

[1] See *The Finding of the Third Eye*.

difficult to admit that the hand may also register memory, both subconscious and conscious, and other knowledge which the ego super-consciously may know about itself or its future. It is said that when a person goes completely insane all lines vanish from the palm of the hand. This seems rather significant! The health, hereditary and physical tendencies are very fully indicated in the hand. A study of palmistry would, I believe, convince many people as to its value, and as to the definite help it could be in diagnoses if used by doctors and psychologists.

Palmistry brings us to the subject of divination, as well as that of prophecy. To foretell any coming event, to interpret any symbol or dream, to unravel any problem or to obtain guidance as to right action in any particular dilemma —all these are in the realm of the subjective, passive, negative forces of the human being. By means of these gifts he (or she) can shift the focus of his conscious attention from the physical plane into the ether, or astral planes, reading there the reflections cast from the mental world, either clairvoyantly or clairaudiently. A person with a talent for so doing usually needs some form of concentration with which to perform the shift of consciousness, preferably something upon which to gaze. Besides its own definite indications the palm of the hand, emitting as it does magnetic rays, is apt to produce the right conditions for divination. Other objects are also conducive, such as a crystal, a bowl of water, even the tea-leaves in a cup or the faces of a pack of cards!

In the second category we can put those practices of an esoteric nature which depend upon the *positive* and active side of the human character, as opposed to the receptive side. Among these we must place magic, both black and white. White magic is the practical and active side of occultism, the concrete result of occult study and training. It depends upon the knowledge and understanding of the 'forces of nature', and the moulding of factors which influence them by the mind under the impetus of the will. Magic entails the creative use of various forces and energies. The only difference between magic and modern science is that in the former case mechanical tools and instruments are either dispensed with or used in conjunction with mental energy creatively wielded.

One of the most well known of magical practices is that of alchemy. This was really the forerunner of chemistry, the alchemist being one who worked with *all* the forces at his disposal instead of with only the lower strata of the physical plane. The alchemists of the Middle Ages had to hide the nature of their esoteric studies and experiments. They often gave out that they were seeking a formula for changing baser metals into gold. Whereas the genuine alchemists were much more interested in discovering how to obtain the Elixir of Life, how to separate and capture that essence of essences which is the stage at which spirit first becomes physical within any body, or at which the physical had been transmuted to the point where it is about to become spiritual. This intermediate linking stage exists within all expressions of life, and constitutes its most potent, vital and creative part. If it is captured it can rejuvenate all grosser tissues and powerfully affect all lower vibrations. The subject of alchemy is a vast one. It holds one of the secrets which are awaiting the attention of a more enlightened humanity. Day by day modern chemistry approaches nearer to the realm of alchemy, with its triturations, high potencies, transmutations, distillations, and the use of electrical energies (instead of the more controlled energy of the mind). Day by day the genuine alchemist labours silent and unknown within our city walls, perfecting his work in the joy of knowledge that the time is nearly ripe for it to be allowed to flower forth for the helping of Aquarian humanity.

The alchemist works with the mineral world, because it is the basis of all physical life. He takes metals, or precious stones which he knows to be the formed bodies of mineral life. Each of these is composed, therefore, of spirit, soul and body —known in his alchemical terminology as mercury (spirit), sulphur (soul), and salt (body). Through a complicated system of distillation, digestion in heat, blending, dividing and reblending, he seeks to hasten the process of mineral evolution and produce the final initiated, transmuted essence of the metal, such as will form the nourishment of evolved humanity of the dimmest future. He seeks to put the metal through its initiations! These include a burning-up of the grosser physical side, a complete separation between body, soul and spirit, and the blending together again of the perfected parts. To accomplish this he must be able to direct rays of spiritual energy through his own mind upon the work he does, and by so doing anticipate his own future as a creative God. True and perfect alchemy is therefore white magic of a high type, coupled with the unutterable patience, accuracy and persistence which is learnt only through the more drab and drudging aspects of life upon this planet.

The practice of alchemy was seriously undertaken by the ancient Egyptians, who left many writings upon it. The Magi studied it in Chaldea, and the ancient Chinese were interested in it also. It is very closely associated with astrology. In the voluminous ancient literature upon alchemy which escaped destruction the secret processes are hinted at in veiled astrological terms.

One of the most celebrated of known alchemists was the Comte de Saint Germain, a description of whose work is give by many writers of his time such as Casanova, to whom he showed a phial of the Water of Paradise, which he had succeeded in producing.

Alchemy is one of those branches of white magic which give physical visible results, producing essences which act powerfully upon physical forms, and actually working in and with some of the densest forms of chemical matter. But there are other forms of white magic which work upon the subtler Planes and produce results which are quite as effective, and in certain respects more so.

The terms 'occult' and 'esoteric' are used to imply a study or understanding of the hidden, invisible sources of manifestation and the laws which govern life. The term 'magic' is applied when this knowledge is deliberately wielded to produce results. The term 'white magic' implies that the magician in question works only from selfless idealistic motives and therefore is able to tap and use high spiritual vibrations. The term 'black magic' implies that the magician in question is personally ambitious, and therefore unable to tune in to and make use of high vibrations. He is obliged to employ the lower astral forces, and enslave the lower entities of the deva world to work for him, through the power of his own animal magnetism. Enslavement being against spiritual law, as well as other practices of black magic, such a magician goes in constant danger of the inevitable Karmic retribution.

Another practice which was fraught with danger, and against the spiritual laws, was that of necromancy. This was a form of divination, or the obtaining of information through calling up the spirits of the dead. Our study of the conditions of the astral plane will enable us to imagine without difficulty the many and various phenomena, mostly horrible, which could occur through this practice, and how unlikely it was that any truly spiritual aid could be gained by thus taking liberties with the individual habits, work and processes through which disincarnated egos must pass. Necromancy might be described as a type of 'Black Spiritualism'!

We have not space to touch on any more of the details of occult practices, and must now enlarge our vision once again and take in the picture as a whole.

We have seen that the invisible structure which underlies, initiates and supports the whole visible fabric of life is formed by the Seven Rays. If we concentrate our attention upon these Rays they will come to have more and more meaning for us. We will be able to use them as a sure clue to the interpreting of and determining upon any fact in manifestation. We must remember that the Rays are cyclic. They are not all in power at once. Each one has its great periods of manifesting power, its giant wave, upon which it rises to its peak, and then gradually sinks again, remaining as a vital undercurrent until the time arrives for it to manifest its work again. These great Ray periods may cover thousands or tens of thousands of years. All the varied complications of life are provided for by the particular combination of Rays which are in power at any given time. When there is great activity in the realms of war and of art we know that the Fourth Ray of Harmony Through Conflict is in power. When humanity is swept by a wave of religious fanaticism and devotion we see the influence of the Sixth Ray. When humanity destroys the old forms and cries out for new we know that the First Ray is there.

Every kingdom in nature is the work of one Ray in particular combining with other Rays in less degree. Every continent, every Race and each nation has its primary and secondary Ray influences. The Egoic Ray of a nation, when known, proclaims the ultimate spiritual achievement of that nation. The Personality Ray governing that nation proclaims the attitude in the physical world by means of which it will attain to its final achievement. The modern study of the Rays is only in its infancy. It requires patience and practice at the beginning, but enough information has already been given out to enable it to be applied very usefully in individual and national psychology and psycho-analysis.[1]

The first law for the spiritual student is, 'Man, know thyself', which includes a knowledge of the whole universe. The second law for the spiritual student, which inevitably takes effect as his vision is enlarged, and is the outcome of achiev-

[1] See *A Treatise on the Seven Rays*.

ing initiation, is 'Man, forget thyself'. The goal of man is from separatism to unity. The first great phase achieved, that of complete integration of the personality, produces the separatist and egotist *par excellence*. The second great stage, that of integration with the soul, kills separatism and produces the sense of duality—the Deity and the soul, soul and spirit, man as a *unit* within a great brotherhood. The third stage, that of integration with spirit, kills duality, producing unity and fusion with the all-consciousness. Man is no longer worshipping God, asking things of God, trying to become like God. He knows that he *is* God, and thinks no more of anything or any creature as being separate from himself. When he touches the fringe of this realisation he can no longer hate or criticise or doubt or despair. He *is*.

Words fail us at this point, but it must ever be remembered that understanding and unity and co-operation with all of life is the final aim of the spiritual aspirant. So long as there is any barrier between himself and any other expression of life, so long as his own life and progress or that of anyone he knows has for him the slightest fraction more importance than any other phase of evolving life, just so long will he remain outside the great revelation and the great fusion.

PART TWO

Review of Material Science

17

The Mineral Kingdom

W<small>HEN</small> we begin to study the structure and composition of the universe, including this planet and all its contents, from the standpoint of material science, we must commence with the statement that the universe is composed of various bodies moving through space at set speeds. These bodies each rotate round their own core, and are electrically polarised. Heat, radiation, rotation, rhythm, an ordered progression through space, and relationship one to another are expressed throughout. Differing degrees of heat, of pressure and of cold, produce varying states which we call solid, liquid and gaseous.

As to the actual matter from which all living form is built up, it is *basically* that which we call mineral, either radiating in highly potentised form or at lower vibration in liquid or solid form. All of this solar system is composed of the same variety of mineral atoms which are present in greater or lesser degree in the various planets. Science shows, through spectral analysis, that the universe is a unity, containing the same substances, subject to the same reactions, which are those of vibration, gravity, heat, movement, light and power. It shows also that these reactions are interchangeable one with another, and transmutable one into another.

Confining our attention for the present to this planet, we learn that the fact of there being a variety of chemical atoms is due to differences in their internal arrangement and vibrationary rate. An atom is found to be composed in the last analysis of energy, this energy being electrical in character. A positive nucleus or proton holds negative electrons within its sphere of influence. This sphere rotates and vibrates at a rate governed by its particular arrangement and its number of electrons. The atom as a whole is either positive or negative, male or female; positive and negative atoms rotate in opposite directions. The valency of an atom means the number of 'hands' by which it can hold on to other atoms, and so form molecules. A 'hand' is an unpaired electron which can be shared with another atom, thus linking the two. Atoms of non-valence are unstable and turn easily to the gaseous state. Atoms with a large number of 'hands' (a large range of valency) can combine to form a variety of organic molecules.

There are ninety-two different kinds of atoms. These give us the ninety-two elementary substances, or the elements from which everything in the world is composed. These are arranged by the scientists in a long scale, according to weight, the weight depending upon the number of positive electrons at the core of an atom. This scale ranges from the lightest, the hydrogen atom, which contains one positive electron as its nucleus, to uranium, the heaviest atom, which contains ninety-two positive electrons at its core.

The ninety-two elements resemble very much the musical scale in their arrangement. They fall into thirteen octaves of seven notes each. An element of a certain 'note' has a definite affinity with the same note in the other octaves of the scale.

The beginnings of sex morality are first seen in the atom. An atom seeks marriage with another atom of opposite polarity. If this is correctly achieved atoms unite to form valuable compounds. Atoms group together and dance round one another to form molecules. According to their valency so can they hold on to one another in various ways, clinging together in square, round, triangular, octagonal, and other formations. Here we see the beginnings of form, for it is the formation of a molecule which determines the structure, density and characteristics of the element or compound formed. Mineral atoms with a large range of valency unite with atoms of acid, and become colloidal (non-crystalline, of gelatinous consistency). Thus is the first step in transmutation begun, because now the colloidal mineral molecule is able to form colloidal substance. From this substance metaplasm is built, and from metaplasm protoplasm is built, from which man's body is formed.

Man's body is built up from combinations of most of the existing elements, some in large quantities and some in infinitesimally small quantities. The mineral in its raw state cannot be absorbed and used by the human being. It would be a poison to him. It has first to be split up and built into subtler compounds by the action upon it of the vegetable kingdom when using it for food. The vegetable kingdom draws the mineral up out of the soil. It draws many elements from out of the air, uses the sun's rays, the moon's rays and other radiations, and by means of this subtle heating and electrifying process performs its alchemy upon the minerals, shedding their coarser lower sheaths, dividing the atoms more finely and building amazing compounds with them, from which cells and tissues can be formed.

When man eats the vegetable kingdom he continues this transmuting process. He forms compounds and substances of an infinitely more subtle and complex nature, until the traces of the original elements are almost lost altogether.

The ninety-two elements are divided into two groups. The first group contains all the metals, which are alkaline, or negative-female in type. The second group contains all the other elements, which are acid, male-positive in type.

These two groups mate with each other, combining to form all the complexities of material existence.

The metal which plays the largest part in this universe is

iron. It exists in tremendous quantities in this planet as well as in others. It has an affinity for oxygen, which is an acid gas composing one-fifth of the air, and readily combines with it to form iron-oxide, a red substance which we know as rust. This combination is repeated in finer form within the human body, the iron drawn from vegetable food combining with the oxygen drawn from the air to form the red substance of the blood.

The properties of oxygen and hydrogen are too well known to describe here, as is also the fact that water is a compound whose molecules are composed of two atoms of hydrogen to one of oxygen. Oxygen and hydrogen are both utterly different from water, yet the marriage of their atoms in these proportions gives us that all-pervading, ever-necessary compound, water, often spoken of as an element.

Another most important element in the acid group is carbon. This exists in large quantities in the earth. It forms the basis of all the compounds which go to make up the forms of living things. In its pure state it is found as the diamond. It is also familiar to us in blacklead, coal and charcoal. As it is the basis of most compounds which make up living forms, it can be recovered as charcoal after the other elements have been driven out by heating or burning.

Calcium is another important metal, which is rarely seen in its pure state. It combines quickly with oxygen. With carbon as a third ingredient it becomes common chalk. Calcium figures very largely in the building of bones and teeth, besides which it is present in all the cells of the body.

Magnesium is a white metal which gives a brilliant light when burning. Its presence in subtle quantities within the bodily cells is quite essential. It stimulates certain of the enzymes, with which we will deal later, into action, helping to build and repair nerve and brain tissues.

Zinc is a metal with which we are quite familiar. It is used to galvanise iron, preventing it from rusting, and therefore must be an element which does not care to combine with oxygen. Zinc is found in all the tissues of the human body, but especially in the gonads and the thyroid gland. As we have mentioned, the creative energy of the body is linked between those two centres, being used in one at the expense of the other.

Copper is another familiar metal. It is an excellent conductor of electricity. Compounds from copper are often light blue in colour. Copper plays an important part in the human body, working with iron for the formation of haemoglobin. It is principally located in the liver.

Phosphorus is an element in the acid group, which is necessary to all living things. In its pure state it is a white solid which glows in the dark, because it is in a rapid state of radiation. In its combined forms it is to be found in considerable quantity in bones, and also as a constituent of the body cells.

Chlorine is another important element in the acidic group. In its pure state it is a pungent yellow gas, used for bleaching and disinfectant action, and also to make poison gas. But it combines readily to form salts. One of its commonest combinations is with sodium to form sodium chloride, which we know as common salt, and which plays a big part in the metabolism of the body.

Sulphur is another acidic element, yellow in colour, from which sulphuric acid is obtained. It combines with sodium to form the salt sodium sulphate which plays an important part in the body.

Iodine is one of the most important of the acidic elements. It exists in a pure state as a black crystal, and in a combined state in the sea in many kinds of seaweed. In the human body it is vitally necessary, because it is an essential constituent of the active principle of the thyroid gland.

Silicon is a very hard transparent element which exists abundantly in the earth's crust. Sand is formed of grains of silicon, which also plays a large part in rock formation. In the human body silicon exists as minute sharp-pointed crystals, which help in the stiffening of the hair, the cell-walls and other tissues of the body.

Sodium is the metal which combines with the acidic chlorine to form common salt. It also combines to form soda and soap. In the human body it controls the supply of water.

Potassium is an extremely important metal which combines readily with oxygen in the open air. Its compounds abound in rich soil and are taken up by the plants. It plays a vital part in the human body.

Hydrogen, the lightest of the elements, belongs to the acidic group, and is necessary to all living things. As stated above, it also forms the compound water in conjunction with oxygen.

That miracle of complexity which differs so much from anything else on earth, the human body, is actually made up from the ninety-two elements,[1] from compounds formed by the marriages between their two groups, the metal alkali (feminine) group and the non-metal acid (masculine) group. These elements combine to form compounds of ever-increasing complexity and ever-heightening vibration, until at last a rhythm is reached which admits of the entry of a certain 'life-element' and the individualised cell appears. In the human body these cells vary considerably, according to whether they are forming bone, flesh, skin, hair, glands or other organs. But in the main they all possess a living nucleus in the centre of the cell which forms it into a coherent entity, having the power of discrimination, selection, growth, propagation and dissolution. A cell has a consciousness which is quite clearly distinguishable to the modern scientist. It may be selfish, greedy, lazy, industrious, sociable or otherwise in varying degree. The cells group themselves together to compose the organs and tissues of the body, forming thus

Of course discoveries will continue as the years pass.—V.S.A.

federations or nations of cells. These soon become motivated by mass desires and moods, and subscribe to the influence of the organ as a whole, just as the public is motivated by its club, its party politic or its national genius.

The cells which form the brain of a human being are, of course, infinitely more subtly composed than those which form the flesh of his arm. The subtilising process increases until the cells as cells become more and more delicate, minute and 'ethereal'. When we come to the brain-cells the physical sources of many of the activities of the brain cannot be traced at all. The material scientist is here rendered somewhat helpless and classifies such activities under the headings of 'energy' and 'electricity'.

After the human body is built up in all its complexity the elements still continue to enter it through the intake of food and air. These elements then induce three functions. The first is a replenishing function, performed by the living cells, which select what they need of the elements and build it into the living fabric of the cell itself. The second function is performed by elements or their compounds moving about *free* within and around the cells, and stimulating various of the organs and cell aggregates to certain activities. The third and vital function of the elements is to preserve the correct balance of electrical polarity within the body, the correct ratio of acid and alkali. This they do by means of interaction between their two groups—metal-alkali and non-metal-acid. In their pure state some of them could not exist in the body at all, and would be rank poisons. But these two groups come together and make marriages, forming into the most wonderful compounds called salts, which between them hold the balance of electrical power steady, and exert strong influences upon all the activities within the body. When these salts are soluble in water they sometimes go under the name of 'electrolytes', which again emphasises their electrical potentialities.

The famous Dr. Schussler studied these salt combinations and formulated a science dealing with them which he called Biochemistry. He stated that salt deficiencies are recognised by various disease symptoms, and replaced by the administration of artificially made cell-salts.

The unorthodox side of this science was further elaborated by Dr. George Carey, who declared that the twelve principal cell-salts in the human body were each produced and activated by one of the Twelve Signs of the Zodiac—that is to say by certain of the Cosmic Rays with which scientists today are struggling to become better acquainted. I have briefly described the theory of the Zodiac and the salts in my last book, together with their actions in the body.[1]

Looking at this theory for one moment, we might say that we know that the cells are living organisms, which explains why they are able to act in various definite ways. But what of the mineral salts existing free within the tissues and exerting each one different influences—so powerful that all the activities of the body depend upon them? Where do those strong influences come from?

We know that most metals are non-conductors of electricity, and that acids are conductors. When the two combine as a salt we then get a carefully balanced polarity which would regulate a flow through them of those forces which we loosely heap under the one word 'electrical'. Is it not reasonable to suppose that all these carefully blended salts could each be the conductor and regulator of the flow through the body of various kinds of rays and energies passing through the atmosphere? This would explain the extreme importance which these metals play in the body, even although in some cases their quantity is so minute as to be hardly traceable. We will talk about this again later.

The orthodox chemist of today states that when a human body has been completely incinerated there remains only the

[1] See *The Finding of the Third Eye*.

non-combustible ash, which represents the mineral constituents in the form of salts. There is about six pounds of this ash. Five-sixths of it is calcium phosphate from the bones. The remaining one pound of ash represents all the other minerals in the body.

Certain of the alkali metal elements, such as potassium, calcium and magnesium, are set opposite such acid elements as phosphorus, chlorine and sulphur to preserve the right ration and prevent 'acidosis' and the grave ills which at once follow any changes in the relative proportions of the elements in the body.

The salts which are free within the body exert what is called osmotic pressure upon the fluids of the body, so that they flow through the cell walls; tissue fluid meets blood fluid and the work of exchange and fetching and carrying thus goes on. The correct balance between the properties and substances of these fluids is thus kept regulated. In a living person the blood is alkaline and the muscles are acid. This separation is held intact by the polarity, or electrical energy, which imbues a living body. At the moment of death the life principle withdraws from the body. The polarity is therefore no longer held and it diffuses, releasing the electricity from the body. The acid and alkali rush together, the blood becomes acid, and all becomes disorganised.

Acid, as we know, stands for male, positive action—the expenditure of energy. Alkali stands for female, negative, passivity—the storing of energy. It is said that the prehistoric animals were alkaline, and therefore without sufficient energy or fight in them to maintain their own survival. They were preyed upon by those animals who developed more acid tendencies. The acid loves to devour the alkaline because of the energy stored within it. Thus the animals devoured the plant life and those more alkaline animals who offered the least resistance.

An energetic person, therefore, whether of mind or of

body, is an acid person—one in whom the acid is inclined to overbalance the alkali proportion. It is the urge within which attracts this superabundance of acid, this acid-forming propensity, and therefore we can rightly say that the state of mind governs metabolism and conditions the body in this important degree at any rate. For if you can get a person suffering from acidosis completely to relax both mentally and physically you will cure him much more quickly than by any other means. A person suffering from auto-intoxication or self-poisoning is one who has generated an excess of acids and mucus in his system through emotion, fatigue, or wrong feeding. Such poisoning may show as a common cold or influenza if the poisons have accumulated in the alimentary or bronchial tracts; as rheumatism or arthritis if the poisons have settled in muscles and bones; or as neuritis if the poisons are located in the nerves. Poison is merely matter in the wrong place or in the wrong proportion. Most disease is said to be directly due, therefore, to a deficiency or superabundance of one of the cell-salts, which will set the others out of gear one by one as they react and work so closely one with another. The result will be a series of symptoms of infinitely varied kinds all over the body. These symptoms have each been given their name by the medical profession, which name has much more to do with the symptom than with the mineral situation in the body which causes it. Such disorganisation in the complicated substances in the body causes new substances to be formed. These often are very welcome food to the variety of microbes which exist in most bodies. Whichever of these microbes can flourish upon the particular abnormal substance produced, proceeds to do so, increases rapidly in numbers, and the result is a so-called infectious disease. There is a school of thought which strongly supports the idea that no infectious disease can be exactly 'caught', but is the result of a condition brought about within the body which is not normal. The body subjects itself to violent reactions in an attempt to re-establish the normal—these reactions are known to us as certain definite diseases. The actual part which microbes do play in the human drama is a mystery which has not yet been elucidated by orthodox science; it would seem to be analogous to the part played in plant life by blight and other insect parasites. The idea that a tree or plant cannot exist without a certain number of these tiny animals has not yet been put forward.

There are, of course, many arguments against the theory that infectious diseases must have their complement within the body before they can be 'caught'. It will be brought forward that in many cases the white man has brought disease germs into a tribe of healthy and beautiful aboriginals, which have wiped out a large percentage of them. To this argument I would say that any aboriginal tribe, however healthy, is pre-eminently super-alkali in its make-up. That is why it has remained an aboriginal tribe! A correct amount of the acid qualities would have ensured a state of active up-to-date 'civilisation' being reached. Such a tribe is in the position of the prehistoric alkaline monsters who could not hold their own against the fast developing acid types. Such a tribe is actually not normal or correctly balanced, and cannot contend with any new acidic microbes, drugs or liquors which the acidic white man may bring with him. In the same way the athlete may run the danger of becoming too alkaline, through taking a non-acidic diet, living a healthy non-acidic life, and not sufficiently using his acid-making brain. Suddenly this splendid specimen will succumb to an unexpected disease, and no one can think why! The cause is always the same—a lack of the correct balance between the mineral salts of his body: *a disturbance, perhaps, of the rhythms of those subtle energies flowing into the body through the medium of the salts.*

We see, therefore, that man's body is founded upon the mineral kingdom, after the latter has been subjected to modifications, and to the action of various rays and energies by the vegetable kingdom, into whose fabric it has been built. We can leave out the animal kingdom entirely in this connection, because man can subsist perfectly well upon the vegetable kingdom alone, but he cannot subsist without it. If he eats meat he is but eating a life which had subsisted upon the vegetables and minerals also.

The mineral kingdom of itself and within itself does not produce cell-life. It takes the impulse and qualities found within the vegetable kingdom to do that. The vegetable kingdom is therefore the great link between the body of the planet, the earth, primal physical matter—and all that which is not of the earth, the rays and energies which radiate down upon and through it. The plant is the link between matter and force, the seen and the unseen, the tangible and the intangible. It weaves and blends these two together to produce itself, and because of this alchemy man is able to exist.

The wisdom teaches that the mineral kingdom is old in its development, that the glorious jewels with their hidden powers are the Initiates of that kingdom, and that the minerals by their powers of radio-activity demonstrate the transmutation which lies ahead for mankind.

18

The Vegetable Kingdom

A VAST and fascinating source of study is offered by the vegetable kingdom. The scientist with his microscope has managed to discover a great deal about it. But much remains yet as a beautiful and tantalising mystery. Scientists have suggested that it was the vegetable kingdom which first set free the oxygen upon this planet, thus making it possible for more advanced life forms to evolve. They say that the heavy carbon-dioxide gas was loosed from the core of the earth as it cooled, and that upon the earth's surface the earliest vegetable forms commenced their long task of splitting up this compound, feeding upon the carbon and setting the oxygen free into the air. Soon there was enough oxygen to support other types of life, and not much carbon-dioxide left for the plants. Animal and insect life then began to appear, breathing in the oxygen and breathing out carbon dioxide. Thus the two kingdoms grew and thrived together, interdependent. The plant draws from the soil the mineral salts that it needs, and from the air the carbon that it needs. It exposes and blends these ingredients to the action of the sun's rays, the moon's rays, and all the other subtle forces in the air. The sun's vibration stimulates the vibrations of the unearthed minerals and the freed carbonic acid gas. Once more we see the meeting of the male acid and the female alkali. Their atoms rush together, their vibrations are raised by the sun's influence, and new and subtler compounds come into existence. The organic cell is formed, the green chloro-phyll comes into being, and the infinite beauties and forms of plant life begin to unfold.

Plant life exists upon and because of certain great currents which intersect one another upon the earth. This planet is negative to the sun, which exerts the law of gravitation upon it. The rays of the sun stream down upon the earth and exert a pulling and drawing influence, drawing up the water from the earth in the form of vapour, drawing up the growing forms upon the earth so that they stand upright and grow towards the sky, drawing upwards the sap within the stem of the plant, the blood within animal and man.

The law of gravitation is also the law of polarity, of the two-way current within a form or between two forms. The sap rises up and flows down along these electric currents, which correspond to the Ida and Pingala currents within the human spine. Scientists have tried to explain by material-istic science what that force is which draws up the sap in a plant but they have not stated that it is due to the polarity between the sun and the earth.

A second current which is necessary to plant life is that which flows from the moon. The moon is often considered as only a reflector of the sun, but it is more than that. It exerts an influence quite its own. Whereas the sun's currents flow in a direction perpendicular to the earth, the moon's currents flow horizontally. This can be recognised when studying their influence upon the ocean tides. The sun's rays give life to the plant; the moon's rays give growth and fructification.[1] A plant exposed to the sun and not the moon will not produce fruit and seed. A plant exposed excessively to moonlight will grow much larger and faster. Seeds planted just be-fore the moon is at the full will produce by far the best results.

[1] The gravitation from the living core of the earth pulls the roots downwards into growth.—V.S.A.

Plants grown to climb on insulated copper wire will do better still, as an extra supply of the electrical forces in the air are thus fed to them. Many other interesting facts such as these could be cited in order to show that the vegetable kingdom, as well as all the other kingdoms in nature, is performing a most complicated alchemy, not only with a few of the chemicals of the earth, but in conjunction with all the forces which play through our solar system, and radiate down from outside our solar system. It has always been the task of genuine scientific astrologers to designate, classify and tabulate these forces and their rhythms and periods, due to interrelative changes in the position of stellar bodies.

Organic life appears when the current of life, the sun's, meets the current of growth, the moon's, and they impinge together upon the matter of the earth. This crossing of the currents has been symbolised for us always in the Cross, which represents matter, the four quarters of the earth, the imprisonment of life within form and the suffering relative to this state.

The vegetable life builds cellulose, starch and sugar from the ingredients at its disposal. Wood is fifty per cent cellulose. Cellulose is convertible into starch, and starch into sugar. The finest of these substances, the sugar, is mostly found in the leaves and flowers of the plant. An unripe banana is mostly starch, whereas an over-ripe banana is mostly sugar. If you pour sulphuric acid over sugar the result is a black mass of charcoal—carbon! Cellulose is the general name given to vegetable fibre or tissue. It consists largely of carbon, hydrogen and oxygen. The modern chemist can imitate nature so well now that he can do almost anything with cellulose. He can convert it into sugar, and then into alcohol. He can produce almost any kind of artificial silk tissue with it, by treating it with heat, with pressure, with acids or alkalis. In this way he is actually imitating those processes which take place in living organisms. The liver, for instance, converts vegetable tissues into sugars, which it stores for use as fuel. When needed this is burnt during bodily activities, and is in this way alcoholised.

Beginning then with a few simple mineral elements which are easily blended one with another, the vegetable kingdom gradually built up an ever-expanding series of more and more subtilised and complicated forms, until it had achieved the strength of the long-lived tree, the fragrance of the rose, the wonder of the orchid, the delicious fruits, the nourishing cereals. It gave to humanity coal, wood, peat— even oil, clothing and food. It is full of surprises and full of mystery. The plant forms produce the most brilliant and exquisite colours and vibrant living perfumes out of the simple ingredients at their disposal. They die, sink into the earth, lose those qualities which they gained from sun, light and life, and, retaining the dark, earthy carbon side of their composition, revert back into manure, peat and, finally, coal. Aeons after, this hard black substance is brought up out of the bowels of the earth, and man in his cleverness brings forth out of it not only all those beautiful brilliant colours again in the form of dyes, but the perfumes too—synthetic, it is true, and somewhat harsh, but recognisable all the same.

The vegetable kingdom suffers the same struggle for exist-ence as the other kingdoms in nature. An interchange of service goes on always between the different species, and they prey upon one another as well. In this way their num-bers are kept in the right ratio. Were it not so, some species of plant might overrun the earth and choke the life out of everything else. Most trees and plants have their own par-ticular parasites, which perform certain valuable functions for those plants. The numbers of these parasites are kept at the right ratio by their being used as food by the birds or by their being preyed upon by larger insects. If anything goes wrong with this arrangement terrible epidemics of these blight occur, and the plant life suffers great depletion.

On the other hand, the plants depend entirely upon certain insects such as bees and moths for pollination and fertilisation. In return they provide honey for the bees and leaf-food for the caterpillars of the moths. The fruit and nut trees depend also upon the larger animals carrying away and eating their harvest, and so scattering the seeds far and wide, and ensuring widespread growth. This latter is one of the natural services which mankind is meant to perform for vegetable life, since he is biologically a fruitarian species.

Furthermore all those living creatures who feed upon the vegetable kingdom set free again some of the minerals in process of digestion, and excrete them once more into the earth, thus replacing those necessities for the future use of the plants. Man, unfortunately, has forgotten the importance of this fact, and has for a long time been sending his sewage into the sea. He has thus gradually impoverished the soil until much of the food he now grows suffers seriously from mineral starvation—and so, as a result, does he.

This shows how the give and take in nature must be fulfilled and how nature is in reality one unity, each section of which depends entirely for one or more necessities of its existence upon one or more of the other sections. If the numbers of one species of animal or plant were not kept down to a certain level by the preying upon it of other species its members would rapidly increase until it exhausted all its food supplies. A disease due to deficiency would soon appear, wipe out large numbers and weaken the rest. There seems to be an inscrutable and watchful intervention on the part of nature to keep the numbers of all living things within bounds. Floods, droughts, earthquakes, plagues and epidemics seem all to be used to reduce living creatures to just a certain number without ever seriously endangering their existence as a species. (I do not refer now to certain tribes and species of animals which are dying out due to their persistent alkaline quality.)

Man himself helps nature as much as he can to keep his own number within bounds. As fast as he triumphs over this or that disease he brings new factors into his life which cause new diseases; short of which he goes to war—or slaughters himself with motor-cars and other gadgets. Unless man and nature worked very hard at his extinction he would soon cover the earth as thickly as grains of sand. The answer to this problem would seem to lie within the realm of eugenics and birth control, and to be within the keeping of a future more controlled and intelligent race. And who knows what the discipline of man in these ways might bring to the other kingdoms? Who can say how much the thoughts and moods of mankind affect and influence the other kingdoms in nature? We are only just on the verge of suspecting that there could reasonably be an answer to this question. Scientists are only beginning to experiment with the effects that the rays of the mind have upon its surroundings, and with the reactions that such stimuli may bring about from metal, from plant and from animal. A few years hence it may not sound so far-fetched to suggest that less greed, less self-indulgence and less cruelty on the part of man will set the pace for a like modification in the habits of all creatures with a less powerful vibration than his own.[1]

Returning to the vegetable kingdom, we see it as a marvellous phenomenon whose beauty is only equalled by its necessity. Without it the earth would be a sandswept desert, in which crude minerals would for ever languish, denied the chance of development, change and radiation. The atoms of earth and of air would mate, but there would be no offspring . . . cell-life would never appear. The great panorama of eternal sacrifice, of give and take between all things —the appearance of the symbolic Cross upon earth is brought about by the appearance of the vegetable kingdom on the earth—is inaugurated when the plant begins its

[1] See *The Secret of Atomic Energy*, by the author.

creative work upon the elements of mineral life, and the energies and fires of nature.

From where did the first cells of the first plants come? This is a question that material scientists cannot answer. Yet there must be an answer. Material science has no answer. Esoteric science has an answer very thoroughly worked out, and utterly fascinating in its many aspects.[1]

[1] See *A Treatise on Cosmic Fire*, by Alice Bailey.

19

The Insect World

THE kingdoms in nature are not well defined. They overlap very subtly, so that there are many types which are halfway between one kingdom, or one species, and another. From the first expression of organic life, a creature composed of one living organic cell, the long chain of evolution is unbroken, until the stage is reached where man appears.

Bacteria really belong in the vegetable kingdom. They range from one-celled creatures to quite complicated little beings. Microbes, viruses and germs all play their amazing parts in the scheme of things. Each present a lifetime's study in itself. Viruses, which are so small that they can hardly be seen under the microscope, are held responsible for such diseases as measles and smallpox. They are suspected also in influenza and the common cold.

Bacteria are larger than viruses, although they are not even as big as a red blood corpuscle. The results of some of their activities are known to us as tuberculosis and pneumonia.

Larger still and more complicated than the bacteria are the protozoa, although they are creatures of only one cell. They cause symptoms which are known as diseases, such as dysentery and malaria.

But the activities of bacteria are not only of an unwelcome nature. They can also be used as a source of very nourishing food. This, I believe, is being already done in Japan. Such forms of bacteria as yeast are well known, as well as the part which they play in cheese, and in alcohol and other fermentations. Bacteria can be nourished on very simple things. Their powers of growth and of multiplying are incredible. Scientists say that if one bacteria were allowed to multiply to its full capacity it would produce a ton of bacteria in a day, and more than the weight of this planet in bacteria in two and a half days! It is possible that much will be done in the future in the way of breeding bacteria food. This might prove to be more productive, possibly, than breeding cattle.

The step between the bacteria world and the insect world is a very subtle one, yet with the insects we step into the animal kingdom. The insects belong in a class called the 'jointed animals', which includes such creatures as crabs and lobsters. So that if an insect is not an animal, then a lobster is an insect! The number of insects on the earth is stupendous. It is estimated that they form half of the animal matter on land. Whereas there are roughly three thousand species of mammals, eight thousand species of fish and ten thousand species of birds, there are far more than two hundred and fifty thousand species of insects. This beats even the vegetable kingdom, of which there are two hundred thousand species known.

Next to the plant kingdom it is probably the insects who play the greatest part in the production of food. It is they who give the greatest aid to the plants, not only by fertilising them, and carrying various bacteria, but by other and subtler chemical actions as well. We hear a lot of complaints about insect pests on crops on a large scale. This has mostly come about through the importation of foreign plants plus their particular parasites, but minus yet other small creatures which keep these within bounds.

Left to itself, it is pretty certain that nature would be capable of regulating all these matters without difficulty. Speaking, as I am in this chapter, in the language of the orthodox scientist or student, I have to talk vaguely of 'nature' in this way, and allow 'nature' to remain a mysterious unexplained and unexplainable something, into the subject of which one goes no further.

It has been found that a pair of small birds, as, for instance, sparrows, carry about two thousand insects to their young every day, besides what they eat themselves. In this way the insects are kept within bounds.

One of the insects which has seriously threatened to usurp more than its share of the earth is the termite. If one wants to get an idea of the almost miraculous manner in which collective action is brought about in the insect world a very good example to study is the termite. This small ant builds strongholds hundreds of tons in weight. The termite as a community seems to live for ever. It is said that this is because the termite is the only living thing which is not deficient in potassium. This is a point to be borne in mind when studying the cell-salts.

The insect kingdom has been exhaustively and patiently studied by scientists. Yet no orthodox scientist can give us the slightest explanation of the extraordinary knowledge, judgment, organisation and foresight, all loosely dumped under the name of 'instinct', which are shown by many insects such as the ant and the bee.

The esotericists have a full explanation of the types of life and evolution which lie behind the insect world, as well as the microbe world.

20

The Animal Kingdom

As we are considering life from the point of view of orthodox science we must include man within the animal kingdom. For in this light man is held to be an animal, plus more highly developed attributes than the animals possess. Darwin's theory that man is descended directly from the apes has still some adherents, although there is a growing school of thought which holds that the monkeys are an offshoot of the original human ancestors. This latter view is held by some of the esotericists, who add that certain tribes of the earliest mankind mated with beasts and the anthropoids were the result.

In this chapter we will consider man as an animal inasmuch as he resembles or is identified with them. Later we will study both resemblances and differences.

The animal kingdom is identified with the plant kingdom in several ways. They both breathe, take in nourishment, grow, propagate, become old and die. But whereas the plant can nourish itself on inorganic matter (minerals which have not been built into cells and become organised into a form) the animal, including man, cannot do this, but relies for food upon organic matter already organised for him by the plant. Of course there are one or two exceptions on the borderline of these classifications, but they do not really count.

Another fundamental difference is that animals are able to move independently about, whereas plants are rooted in their soil, or at any rate not capable of self-initiated movement from one place to another.

A plant has the power of discrimination, choice, self-modification under external influences, and is sensitive to the radiations caused by all the activities around it, to the point of showing both pleasure and pain. An animal possesses all these characteristics, much further developed, plus the power to feel intense emotion, such as fear, rage, devotion and joy. The animals seem to be guided by a certain remarkable intelligence which instructs them unerringly in such matters as migrating in the direction of food and warmth, mating and bringing up their young, and resorting to ingenious subterfuges to protect their species. This mentality guides the animal in much the same way as a sleep-walker is guided, without the factor of self-consciousness, and apparently all the more surely for that reason. This mentality is loosely grouped by orthodox science under the headings of 'instinct', although the scientist does not say what it is, where it dwells, or why it is in some ways superior and in some ways inferior to the intelligence of well-developed men.

In the higher types of animals it is possible to develop a rudimentary reasoning power and a keen memory. An intimate association with mankind appears to awaken in many of them the germs of self-consciousness and individual creative or inventive power. This brings us to the actual difference existing between man and animal. It is creative power and a consciousness of the separate self. Man possesses all that the animal possesses, including that 'sleep-walking' mentality called instinct, which can, if allowed free play, protect and guide him in all the activities of his physical life.

But he also possesses another kind of mind as well, which is individual, that is to say different in each man, and which is capable of *unlimited unfoldment and outward expression*. We do not know of how much the animals are aware. For all we can tell they may be in communion with life forces or intelligences of which we know nothing. But we do know that they cannot express whatever knowledge they may have creatively in arts and sciences. How did this vital difference which exists between man and ape begin; from where did it come? If it grew gradually in prehistoric man, why did it not grow in the ape as well, and in other animals? Orthodox science has no answer to this question, and is not yet prepared to consider the full explanations given by esoteric science.

Animal life began, according to the biologists, with single-celled animals living in water. The single-cell creature is called the protozoon. Then came the metazoa, or organisms of multiple cells. These were later organised into the morula or mulberry forms. Finally the cells were able to organise into a hollow spherical form called the blastula. A further development produced a hollow indented ball, formed of an inner, middle and outer layer. This latter is called the gastrula. We can see an example of it in the egg of a fish.

At this stage evolution had produced a complicated cell from which could be produced a complicated corm built up of many ingredients. The outer layer of the gastrula, the ectoderm, was able to develop hair, skin, spinal cord, nerves and brain. The inner layer, the endoderm, can develop the digestive organs, the liver and the lungs. The middle layer, the mesoblast, can develop bones, muscles, ligaments and blood-vessels.

The gradual stages through which, during millions of years, the evolving life has built forms ranging from protozoa to man can be readily traced to this day. The most complex form of life still begins with one cell. The historical stages of development are recapitulated in each separate growing embryo, the most perfect recapitulation of all being within the human embryo.

A favourite example of recapitulation of the stages of

animal evolution is found in the frog. The embryonic frog starts as a protozoon, then builds up into metazoa, then morula, then blastula, and finally gastrula, the completed egg. The egg is hatched out into the tadpole. This is actually a fish, having gills and no lungs. It has the vertebrae and the heart of a fish, and has neither teeth nor tongue.

The tadpole, however, does not remain a fish, but recapitulates the further historical animal development. It develops limbs, lungs and a tongue, and can now breathe both air and water. At this stage it is called a siren.

The siren continues to develop, producing a vascular system and blood, and a three-chambered heart, and so becoming an amphibian, or an animal who lives partly on land and partly on water. At this stage the siren has changed into the triton.

The triton continues further to develop his lungs for air, grows teeth, and finally becomes an insectivorous land animal, the frog. During this remarkable development this unique animal has recapitulated within a few days more than 45 million years of history.

In the human embryo the same process is gone through, beginning with the protozoa, and carrying on from the frog stage through further animal development until the ape stage is reached. At that point it is said to be impossible to tell the difference between the embryo of a human being or that of an ape or even of a deer. If a great shock through fright or accident is applied to the human embryo while it is at any of these stages, sufficient to cause arrested development, a creature is brought to birth corresponding to the interrupted stage. Besides physical characteristics, the physiological characteristics pertaining particularly to these different animal forms are also involved.

Character has been slowly built up through the addition, in animal evolution, of one attribute and form shape after another, each giving further capacity for feeling and reacting. Each succeeding animal form contains within itself not only the recapitulation of form evolution but of character evolution also. The higher animals contain the sum of the memories, instincts, feelings and qualities of those which came before, plus that particular quality which it adds as its contribution to the whole. Man, the final flowering of the evolutionary process, contains within himself the potentialities of the metal and the plant, the tiger and the bear, the dove and the bee—plus that great something which is his unique contribution to the carrying forward of evolution.

All the four kingdoms, mineral, vegetable, animal, and man, are intimately interwoven with each other in their lives, not only in the questions of nourishment and other mutual aids, but actually in their internal composition. The whole pattern of life is woven of the same threads, evolution and advancement producing merely additional threads blended with those already in use.

The highest branch of animals are those with a backbone. The highest division of that branch are the warm-blooded mammals. The long ladder of animal evolution begins with animals which are one-celled when adult, and continues through various classes such as the earth-worms, sponges, sea-anemones, oysters, snails and insects, until the stage is reached where a backbone is built. From there on come the reptiles, fish, birds, and then all the four-legged animals, the great mammal class which embraces man himself.

Most of the larger, stronger, and more intelligent animals are vegetarians. These include the cattle, sheep, horses, elephants, etc.; the strongest jungle animal, and perhaps the most independent, is the gorilla. He belongs to the *fruitarian species,* and, biologically, *so does man,* his nearest relative. This is what science states and proves.

But it cannot be denied that man, through curiosity, greed and indulgence, fell from his natural fruitarian state, descending to a vicious circle of unnatural living which finally included all types of flesh-eating and false stimulants, and stupefying cooked 'nourishment'. He thus betrayed his function on this planet, and created the Dark Ages of ignorance, disease, famine and warfare.

Through untold generations he so conditioned himself to unnatural and predatory living that he can now hardly imagine a humanitarian and fruitarian civilization (the Garden of Eden!). Yet history tells us that when the Romans discovered the early Britons and paraded them in Roman cities, they were given the name of 'angels' because of their beautiful appearance, and it was discovered that their nourishment consisted chiefly of raw wild berries, nuts and fresh water. During the golden period of the early Greeks, when their physical perfection and prowess in speed and warfare were the envy of all, it was known that they relied for their strength on a diet of the red wild apples of the Greek forests.

Today, hundreds of diseased people, pronounced incurable by the medical profession, have been cured by systems of fasting and fruitarianism. Esoteric teachings declare that only through a harmless diet from the plant kingdom will man reach his divine inheritance, and restore peace and plenty upon earth. Can we imagine what the results will be on health in animal plant and man, on economic, social and international conditions, when mankind eventually lives according to Divine plan?

21

The Endocrine Glands

WE can now pass to the most recent and significant branch of medical study, that of the endocrine glands. It is not necessary for our present purpose to outline the general formation and processes of the human body; there are dozens of medical or anatomical books which may be referred to for this.

The glands, however, are the very crux of the human make-up, and their extreme importance has only quite lately been discovered by orthodox science. It is now known that they are the actual determiners of the type of body, character and mentality of the individual. They are like little specialising chemists who manufacture a variety of subtle and vital secretions which are poured into the blood-stream at a rate determined by them. These secretions provide the foundation for bodily metabolism and the substances utilised for various thought processes. Scientists are agreed that the body and personality are 'run by the glands'. The cry has gone up that a man is what his glands are, and that his whole disposition can be altered by injections into and operations upon these glands. One might perhaps just as well say that a starving man's character can be altered by giving him food, or a suffocating man's nature may be instantly changed by giving him oxygen. For glandular disturbance is usually due to deficiency or starvation on the part of some gland. Even in the case of overactivity of a gland, this is due to starvation of another gland which should be acting as a check upon it.

There can be severe glandular deficiency even when the intake of food and air is quite adequate. If we ask ourselves what is the causative force behind the glands—'The glands run the body, but who or what runs them?'—the reply is likely to be nebulous. It is known that the glands do affect the mental processes, so it cannot be said that the mind or brain actually controls them. Orthodox science has not yet brought itself seriously to consider the soul or ego as a factor in medical science, although tentative suggestions in this direction can already be traced here and there.

That the mind processes are controlled by the ego (or that spark of life which coheres the whole individual) is granted by certain of the psychologists, but that the ego should also be in control of the glandular system and influence it through the mind is something which lies ahead for future amplification. The question from where the glands obtain the forces and ingredients and capacities with which to perform their most subtle alchemies is still unanswered. The plant performs like marvels through using sunlight, moonlight and other rays which pass through upon the ethers.

When psychologists are ready to accept the ego or soul, and then perforce consult the soul-sciences, or the Ageless Wisdom, they will find a full exposition given—of how the etheric body contains these vortices or 'centres', which specifically collect each their particular electrical, or solar force, ray or energy to pass it directly into the gland which it feeds—and of how these centres have their duplicates in the emotional and mental bodies or sheaths—then the reactions and interdependence of these factors will be understood in their right sequence.

How is it that, in apparently identical conditions, in one case a glandular operation will be a success and in another it will be a failure? In an animal, where the individual or egoic factor does not enter in to any considerable extent, the results of glandular experiments are mostly invariable and automatic. But in the human being the element of extreme uncertainty always enters in. This would suggest the necessity for further analysis of some factor in the human which differs from the animal—the soul or ego !

The principal endocrine glands are the pineal, pituitary, thyroid, thymus, pancreas, adrenals and gonads. There is a perfect correspondence here with the seven 'psychic' centres which have been named and described in the Ageless Wisdom in many tongues and for many thousands of years, and whose positions in the body are identical, or almost so, with those of the seven principal glands.[1]

The pineal gland is situated in the middle of the head. Its function is to inaugurate the work of the other glands, and to regulate the action of light upon the body. It has been ascertained scientifically that it was once a third eye. It acts as a check upon the adrenals, so that, if it is deficient, precocious development in the child ensues. Esoterically, it is said to be fed by the 'centre' which is the channel for spiritual or egoic force. Although it is recessional or inactive after adolescence, the stimulation of the highest processes of thinking will bring it into activity again in later life.

The pituitary body is situated in the head in front of the pineal, behind the root of the nose. It is a double gland. The physiological function of its frontal lobe is to pour tethalin into the blood for the stimulation of bone and muscle growth. The posterior lobe pours pituitrin into the spinal fluid for the toning up of the tissues and the lower organs. Overaction of the pituitary gives elongation of the bones and giantism. Complete loss of its functions would result in death from cold in three days.

Psychologically, the pituitary powerfully affects the intellect. Its frontal lobe stimulates the frontal lobe of the brain to engage in abstract thought, logic, mathematics and art. Its posterior lobe acts upon the base of the brain, the seat of

[1] See *The Finding of the Third Eye.*

emotional control and co-ordination. It stimulates sympathy, sociability, poetry and idealism. A large pituitary gives high blood-pressure, great mental and sex activity and initiative. A deficient pituitary results in lethargy and lack of control.

Esoterically, the pituitary body is the seat of the Ajna centre. This is the channel through which the collected impressions from the astral, etheric and lower mental planes are brought into position for their illumination by the spirit, and their direction by the ego, through the channel of the pineal 'centre' and the uppermost head centre. These collected impressions are drawn up from the lower centres of the body by the magnetism of its highest rates of vibration, which are centred in the head. The centres fuse in interchangeable sets of threes, called triangles. They produce a triangle first in the centres which are channels for the physical forces, secondly in the centres which are channels for the astral forces, and thirdly in the centres which are channels for the mental forces. The forces playing through the lower triangles are stepped up in set stages into the higher triangles, and so brought in time in a concerted form up to the control of the egoic centre in the head. The interaction of the centres is analogous to the interaction observable by physicians in their corresponding endocrine glands.

The thyroid gland is located in the throat. It produces thyroxin. This secretion is a lubricator of the nerves and muscles, increasing their conductivity and responsiveness, accelerating metabolism, and thus increasing the speed of living. Through its action great assistance is given to the transforming of chemical materials into energy for the use of feeling, action and thought. It makes possible quick thought-associations and active memory, thus giving the individual power for complex thought, habit formation, and interaction between all the nerves and the brain.

Thyroid deficiency results in the body growing up, while the ego remains infantile, without any moral sense, and no creative capacity either sexually or mentally. It can produce a cretin.

Thyroid over-activity may cause the individual to pass rapidly into maturity while retaining the body and brain of a midget. In a lesser degree it may produce goitre.

Within the thyroid glands are the parathyroids, tiny bodies which act as a brake upon the energy-producing thyroids. The parathyroids are non-conductors of energy. They regulate the amount of calcium in the body, which latter inhibits the flow of excess energy.

Psychologically, a very active thyroid increases sensitivity, rendering one extremely susceptible to all sensation, energetic and talkative. In extreme cases it can lead to megalomania. A deficiency of thyroid secretion renders one lazy, ashamed, seclusive and of poor perception. Irregular thyroidism gives moodiness. Continual stimulation of the throat and thyroid gives the emotional excitability found in singers.

Esoterically, the throat centre is the vitally important centre which the ego uses for creative work. Just as the Deity created by the Word, so does the microcosm, man, after bringing together all his impressions, energies and inspirations under the will of the ego, show forth the result through the energy of the throat centre, no matter what form it takes. Thus a disturbance in the function of the thyroid may be caused by a lack of iodine for the manufacture of thyroxin— but it may also be caused by a lack of creative work, especially in a celibate, or in one with an excess of unused creative energy.

The thymus gland is situated in the chest. It dominates childhood, and its function is to grow the body. Until this is done it holds in check the growth of the other glands. At puberty the sex glands take over control and the thymus should recede. If the sex glands are weak and the thymus remains in power, continued childishness of character is the result. This produces a person who is timid, credulous and full of charm. Such people can easily die of shock.

Esoterically, the centre near the thymus is that connected with the heart, called the heart centre. It is the channel through which the wisdom of the soul, that of the second ray, flows. Just as the first ray energy, that of spiritual will, flows through the upper head centre, the third ray aspect, the personality force, flows through the centres below the heart centre. Wisdom must be linked to will and activity to make a complete creative whole. So the personality force must be raised to the heart force. When that is awakened, all must be raised and linked to the spiritual force, which flows down through the thousand-petalled-lotus centre at the top of the head into the pineal gland. 'As a man thinketh *in his heart, so is he*'! These were words giving a hint of the wisdom which may flow through the channel of the awakened heart centre.

The solar plexus must come next under our consideration. This great network of nerves and blood-vessels which feed the digestive system is of the very utmost importance. It is the receiving set, or brain, of the body, registering impressions from many sources, and reacting violently to them. The pancreas plays a big part in the midst of this complicated area, being a gland which acts as a capitalist! It works to secure the conservation of sugar for use in the expenditure of energy, by converting it into glycogen and storing it in the liver.

Esoterically, the solar plexus can be used as a second brain under certain circumstances, such as fasting. Through it sight is possible upon the physical plane, and also upon the etheric, as well as hearing. This is because the astral body has its roots in the liver, and some of the more vital of the etheric currents flow through it. The impact of any shock or fright is felt in the solar plexus, and it at once inhibits or deranges digestive functions. The solar plexus 'centre' is situated in the spleen. It forms a channel through which solar radiations are concentrated into the spleen in the medium of the ether. The solar plexus region is the great clearing-house of the emotions and other feelings of the lower personality.

The adrenals are small double glands above the kidneys. They are the users of energy, the drivers of the bodily mechanism. They ensure a full blood supply to the muscles. They secrete adrenalin, an extra supply of which is poured into the blood in moments of fright, emergency or combat. Adrenalin speeds up all the sensitivities and muscular reactions of the body, frees an extra supply of sugar and produces a temporary state of high-speed living.

Modern civilisation exerts a continual drain upon the adrenals by reason of the perpetual states of tension, worry, over-stimulation and hurry which it fosters. This results in various types of breakdown, mental, nervous and muscular, especially if the effects are reinforced by an excitable thyroid. The steadying and controlling influence of a well-developed pituitary is the best remedy for this state of things. This is achieved by cultivating especially its powers for abstract unemotional thought, as found in mathematics, logic and philosophy. A serious study, for instance, of the Ageless Wisdom, coupled with exercises in slow breathing, would constitute a sure remedy for certain types of neurasthenia and exhaustion.

Psychologically, it can be said that the adrenals produce reaction to environment, and the reactions of self-protection. When danger threatens they inhibit every other function of the body so as to concentrate it upon the immediate need. The cortex of the adrenals, which regulates secondary sex characteristics, produces the attitude of fight. The medulla produces the necessary warning attitude of fright, and speeds up the metabolism. Whether the individual resulting is a coward or a bully, or a well-balanced man, depends upon the particular type of interplay that there is with the other glands.

Esoterically, the 'centre' connected with the adrenals is the second of the lower triangle, and is the channel for those forces which feed the so-called animal nature. The aspirant aims always at transmuting these forces to higher vibrations.

The chief function of the gonads is that of propagation or creation. They produce potent essences which act creatively wherever they are found within the body. These essences are used in inspirational mental or creative work, and, when thus used, regulate and control the propagative instinct. Unnatural excesses in the latter case starve the organs of the brain, and mental defectiveness or imbecility is often the result.

The gonads are situated near the base of the spine. In this locality is to be found the lowest and first of the 'centres', where sleeps the Kundalini, the coiled serpent of fire, of whom we have spoken before.[1] Into this channel flow the fires of the physical plane, those electrical, magnetic forces which, until they have been transmuted by mating with their polar opposite in the head, are blind, uncontrolled, and therefore best left to sleep until, in the natural course of events, the spirit calls them up.

Thus briefly sketched in is an outline of the principal glands and their connection with the principal 'centres'. Volumes might be written of what is known about all of them, but in this chapter I only want to point out their obvious relationship. Specialists of the endocrine glands claim to recognise the glandular types on sight. An individual may be ruled by one particular gland, which may in time cede its rulership to another of the glands. There are pituitary-centred, thyroid-centred or adrenal-centred types. These can be recognised by their skin, hair, teeth, eyes, colouring, stature and skeleton type, as well as by their psychological characteristics.

If there are deficiencies or abnormalities in the glandular workings they can often successfully be remedied by means

[1] See *The Finding of the Third Eye*.

of injections, electrical stimulation or operations. By this means it has been possible to transform an imbecile or dwarf into a normal being. But once the glands are functioning normally it is more difficult to say what it actually is which causes each gland to function in a different way. For each one has the power to manufacture a most subtle and complex secretion peculiar to itself, and to regulate to a correct degree the discharge of that secretion into the blood-stream.

Esotericists explain it in this way. They say that man is a tiny replica, in the electrical sense, of the solar system; that his endocrine glands are a repetition of the planets; that his centres are a repetition of the centres which feed the planets; that each respectively has its vibrational chord, or belongs on one of the rays; and that the miniature replica is therefore fed by the self-same rays, emanations or energies which flow through its greater counterpart. Each planet performs its own particular metabolism with its own particular mineral make-up. This is subtly repeated in the respective gland in man, which works in conjunction with one or more of the cell-salts. The cell-salts have formed compounds, such as calcium-phosphate, which, it is said, are brought together through the interplay of a certain zodiacal-sign radiation with a certain planetary radiation. Much has been written about this difficult science, still in its infancy, and statistics and proofs are in process of being collected.

It is probable that a knowledge of a man's rays, and an understanding of the effect which that particular assortment was having upon their respective glands, would explain much of the hidden workings of his body, and give the clue to psychological and other gland treatments, which would obviate guesswork. It is certain that when the cosmic rays, and the other rays and energies which are pouring through each human being, are better understood, and their relationship to those vital cell-salts is realised, a new era of medical science will have dawned.

22

The Electrical Kingdom

Under the term 'electrical' we will at this stage class the whole world of invisible energies, rays and radiations, as known and tabulated by modern orthodox science.

The tiny particles which race round the nucleus of any atom are called electrons because they are found to be composed purely of a charge of 'electricity' (I put the word in inverted commas because it is so loosely used) negatively polarised. The particles forming the nucleus of the atom are said to be charges of 'electricity' positively polarised. The forces at work within atoms, their living processes and their motion, cause certain particles continually to escape from their peripheries and shoot off into space. The numbers of these particles which are being shot off from every atom in the whole universe all the time cannot be imagined. But they all contribute to form some of the electrical constituents of the atmosphere.

When we talk about the electron being a particle of negative electricity we must remember that the particle itself could not exist as a cohesive entity unless it were held together by polar attraction. It is therefore composed of still smaller positive and negative electrical particles, which must also be liable to escape and change. The scientist has to stop his discoveries when his calculations, his instruments and his microscopes can no longer deal with the infinite smallness. But nature does not need to stop at this point. We have no reason to state that the particles composing a particle within an atom are by any means the smallest particles in existence. Nor have we any right to state that an electron is purely a particle of electricity. In view of the fact that every cohesive body larger than an electron is composite in character, we must assume that the electron is composite also. We must even assume that the particles which compose the electron (or the proton) must each be composite too !

Now, a thing which is composite is compounded of various ingredients. It is therefore not enough to say that the electrons in an atom are each simple identical charges of 'electricity'. It is more reasonable to infer that they have each a different function and place within the atom, and are composed of a differing material or of a differing compound of ingredients one to the other. The planets which swing round the sun vary entirely in their composition, speed, temperature and principal ingredients, this difference being largely determined by their distance from the sun. The electrons, which we are told swing each in its own orbit around the sun or nucleus of the atom, must therefore be each equally different one from the other. The planets themselves are very composite, formed of a variety of ingredients. We have no right to suppose that each tiny electron is any less composite, or contains any fewer ingredients !

Now, what can possibly be the nature of ingredients so minute as to make up the body of a particle within the body of an electron ? They must, of course, all come under our very elastic heading of 'electrical', but they must all be, nevertheless, essentially different in their character. When we have determined the secret of *what* these minute ingredients really are we are getting far nearer to determining the *basic* factors which are moulding all forms of life.

Out of the ingenuity of his own mind man found how to harness and control electricity, how to capture it, condense it, store it and discharge it again for specific purposes. When he produced his insulators, his coils and his oscillating circuits he was entirely unaware that he was making a replica of an instrument which was already at work within every tiny cell in his body!

The published results of Georges Lakhovsky's researches into the life and energy of the cell are as follows. Within the nucleus of the cell are some minute banana-shaped bodies. These are composed of a microscopic coiled filament whose outer surface is formed of a non-conductive (or insulating) material. This is formed from the acid group of elements, while the filament itself is composed of metallic conductive material. Within the filament tube is contained a fluid, which is conductive in character, and contains all the mineral salts found in sea-water. Here we have a perfect electrical oscillating circuit, capable of self-inductance (auto-storage of electricity) on a microscopic scale. 'Electrical' energy passes through this circuit, is stored, and then begins to discharge. Each discharge is an oscillation (vibration) which sets up its respective wave in the ether.

The oscillation and wave-length of the cell depend upon the arrangement, shape and length of the filaments and their fluid content. These must differ in every cell, because every type of cell in a human body, for instance, has a different wave-length, or rate of vibration. This is in accordance with the statement that every cell has its own conscious individuality.

The individual wave-length of the cell is one of extremely high frequency because of its tiny size. We must now ask whether there are in existence any known rays of energies which could feed so minute an accumulator as that within the cell.

This brings us to the question of the cosmic rays, which have been the subject of widespread investigation in recent years. The cosmic rays are radiations which are emanated from far distant sources in the universe. They strike this planet from all directions, penetrating the surface to various degrees, according to their frequencies.

The wave-length and frequency of oscillation of X-rays is inconceivably shorter and quicker than those of wireless waves. The wave-length and frequency of most cosmic waves is inconceivably shorter and quicker than those of the X-ray.

Cosmic waves have a higher frequency and a shorter wave-length than any other radiations known to us. Therefore they can penetrate deeper into water or solid matter than any other rays. They can also affect the tiniest atoms within the cells more definitely than any grosser radiations could, being able to split them up to transmute them.

There are a tremendous number of cosmic rays. According to Georges Lakhovsky it has been ascertained that their wavelengths correspond to the wave-lengths of the living cell, not only by reason of their extreme shortness and their relative frequency, but also because there would appear to be a corresponding cosmic wave-length to each single different cell wave-length of the uncounted millions in existence.

It seems from this as if we are on the track of those subtle influences which keep life in perpetual motion and infinite differentiation, and that these influences emanate from outside this planet altogether, and even from outside this solar system. The cosmic ray, according to many opinions, bears electric particles such as electrons and protons, which have apparently been radiated off from some far-distant centre. As radiation presupposes a body, with some type of electrical discharge from its centre, and as such a body or bodies could only be stellar in character, we may conclude that certain (or many) of the stars of the universe are helping to run life on this planet. Apparently it is the rays of higher frequency which play the most important part, because of their intimate action within the first minute differentiations of matter which are the basis of physical life. We can say, therefore, that those subtlest rays of the cosmos are possibly more vitally important in our life than those of the sun and the nearer planets of this solar system.

By comparison with such far-distant ray-sources, the potency of the nearer emanations of planets such as Jupiter and Venus must now be a foregone conclusion. When we picture, also, the many cross-currents of rays which intersect one another at various angles at various times, according to planetary movements, thus performing interstellar alchemy, we cannot fail to realise that astrology attempts to deal with perfectly tangible realities. Furthermore, we must remember that to reflect a ray nearly doubles its strength. The moon reflects a large number of rays on to the earth, during the night, when their frequencies cannot be inducted by the powerful sun's rays. If we consider what power they thus must have we can no longer listen to people who deny the power of the moon. Furthermore, the different phases of the moon must obviously reflect an entirely different modification of rays.

The work that is being done by modern scientists and researchers is bringing so much to light so rapidly that it is difficult immediately to measure its significance. The statement that it is the filament circuits forming the nucleus of the cell which determine, by infinite variations in their arrangement and structure, the ultimate nature of the cell, must be connected with another fact. This is that when the cell divides into two it is these filaments, under the name of chromosomes, which divide into halves to form the two nuclei of the daughter cells. To these nuclei are now attributed the conserving of hereditary characteristics. *Heredity would thus be closely associated with a certain wave-length.* We can see a link here with the importance which scientists of old have always attached to numbers and their significance.

Modern researchers have sketched and photographed the electrical oscillating circuits which are the life of the cell.

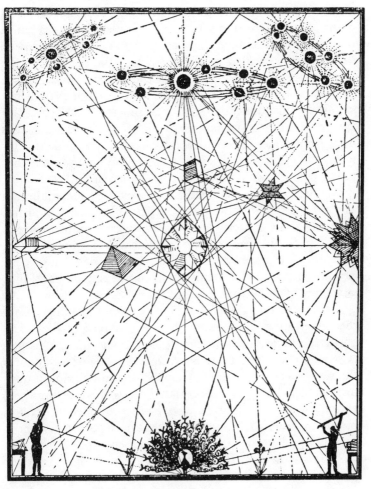

The Scientist and the Astrologer

There was one scientist at least, of last century, who went further than that! This was the famous Dr. Edwin Babbitt. In his *Principles of Light and Colour,* published in 1878, he gives an intricate drawing of an atom from an electrical point of view. He shows in this a complex system of spiral filaments which conduct and store the flow of electricity of *differing types* which passes in through the medium of the various ethers. He shows also how the electrical and thermal colours of the spectrum are expressed through the various spirals. In this connection it is interesting to note that recently the *colours* of the radiations given off by atoms and cells have been under observation by scientists. Dr. Crile, for instance, the inventor of heavy water, has demonstrated that visible colour radiations are emitted by the brain.

Dr. Babbitt held that transparent coloured material, such as glass, selected and attracted particles of the particular ray or rays in the atmosphere whose mineral content agreed with the frequency, or vibrational rate, of the colour in question. He claimed that through red glass one could capture and pass the infinitesimal particles containing iron which are propelled upon certain rays.

He worked out a system of healing upon these lines, using the penetrating qualities of the rays to project these fine particles of various minerals deep into the human tissues. Although it was said that his treatments achieved many cures the time was not ripe for such a subtle and delicate form of natural healing to be appreciated. It was soon forgotten, except by a few pioneers who have continued the work, mostly in America. I understand that in the State Asylum of Chicago patients are treated by sound, colour and perfume. In Kansas there is Dr. Kolar, who uses colour to induce hypnosis or anaesthesia of a certain kind, during which he can perform delicate operations upon his patients while they remain fully conscious. Dr. Radwan, of Vienna, treated his patients by sound, inducing trance and psycho-analytic conditions through the use of certain phonograph records.

Extensive experiments upon the effects to be obtained by the scientific use of sound, colour and perfume, either together or singly, have been in progress for some time. In their final analysis they are really experiments with oscillation and ray energies. Use is being made of many of the unknown cosmic rays in these ways, bringing into play the fact that by reason of their extremely high frequency and short wavelength they can affect living tissues at their very source by acting directly upon the *nuclei* of the cells. All vibratory phenomena, such as sound, colour and perfume, are necessarily the most direct channels by which the cosmic rays may be reached.

A fourth method is that of stimulating or altering existing rates of vibration through the application of artificially induced oscillation. Dr. Babbitt had a colleague who preferred to try this latter means instead of using colour. This was Dr. Abrams, who invented the famous Abrams Box.

This instrument was designed to diagnose disease on the theory that all illness was due to a disturbance of the normal vibrations of the cells. The human being was treated rather like a wireless set. A table of the vibrational-numbers of his various organs and tissues was made, as well as one with the vibrational-numbers of various well-known diseases. When the abnormal vibration in a patient was ascertained the cure was attempted by cutting out or short-circuiting this vibration by putting a stronger complementary one through the patient from the machine.

Such a method of healing, being in its infancy, was subjected to much scorn. It was carried forward by only a few courageous non-orthodox practitioners. Of late it has been much changed and improved, and new instruments, built upon the same theories of vibration, have been invented.

The latest and most successful of these would appear to be the multiple wave oscillator invented by Georges Lakhovsky.

This consists of a whole series of circuits slung together and so graded that every single wave-length in the whole gamut of rays, down to the shortest of the cosmic wave-lengths, can be absorbed and transmitted. When a living human organism is near to this multiple oscillator, the cells do their own healing by absorbing whichever stimulating vibrations they need. A general recovery in health is said to be the first effect, followed by the return to normal of any particular disease symptoms. In this instance no foreign matter or foreign vibrations are forcibly injected into the human tissue, as in the case of X-ray and radium treatment. Therefore one may expect that this instrument will turn out to be an improvement upon other methods of healing. The work is actually left to the little subtle engineers and chemists within the human body.

In America and other countries scientists such as Dr. Ruth Drown are occupied with the completion of inventions just as wonderful. It is claimed that it is possible to obtain a photograph of the physical condition of the whole body of the patient, however far away he may be, if he sends one drop of his blood to be inserted into a photographic instrument. The drop of blood acts as a miniature receiving station to the rest of the body, however many miles away it may be, and by its means the photograph is 'wirelessed', as it were.

With the patient present a photograph may be taken of his interior processes, without light of any kind, utilising the radiatory electrical light of the cells of the body as illumination. The author has examined many of these photographic plates, some of which showed the interior of the brain with the rays of light which are emitted in thinking.

The use of highly potentised and triturated medicines reveals an instinctive effort to utilise the finest particles of substance obtainable; in other words, that part of the substance which is nearest the realm of the radiations and rays at work within it. This science (homeopathy) was developed after it was accidentally discovered what an extremely powerful effect such minute doses exercised.

Lakhovsky[1] and other modern researchers agree with Dr. Babbitt in stating that disease occurs when the normal vibration of any cells is altered. This brings about disequilibrium, and causes daughter cells of the wrong frequency to be produced. This change of vibration may be brought about by microbes whose own vibration is stronger than the particular cell or cells which they contact. Or it may be brought about by too much, or unbalanced, activity of mineral radiation. This we have already considered when dealing with the mineral salts of the body. But Lakhovsky has discovered that there can be a further kind of unbalanced radiation, occurring outside the body on the surface of the earth. Mineral constituents are distributed irregularly within the surface of the earth. Some of them refract the cosmic rays, while others absorb them. Refraction causes criss-cross vibrations, or 'interruptions', to be set up. These apparently affect the human organism, upsetting normal cell-life and producing one of the causes which help to bring about cancer and other diseases. Statistics have proved that cancer is most highly prevalent on certain soils, of which clay soil is one of the foremost.

These interesting new hypotheses have apparently been proven to be correct, principally by the way in which the remedies prescribed have been immediately effective. These remedies were calculated to control the cosmic radiation in the vicinity of the patient. During the last few years, therefore, a tremendous new field has been opened up in the realm of electricity, magnetism and radiations, which is bound to lead to fascinating and far-reaching developments in the future.

It is not only upon the human kingdom, however, that the effects of all these subtle energies are being observed. It is

[1] *The Secret of Life*, by Georges Lakhovsky.

coming more and more to be realised that all existing cellular life is run by cosmic and planetary rays through their representatives here on earth—the minerals. When the mineral in its finest and subtlest form—the cosmic ray—reaches the mineral in its grossest form in the earth state, interaction is immediately set up, and the process of physical evolution begins. Interaction continues until a condition of combining and blending has been attained sufficient to allow an organic cell to be formed. This marks the change from inorganic to organic life. From then on living, growing, propagating forms can evolve. It has been demonstrated what tremendous influence the rays have upon plant growth. In particular the different effects which the phases of the moon have upon plant life have been the subject of careful experiments. Madame Kolisko contributed valuable work of this type, obtaining remarkable photographs of the effect of different planetary configurations upon plant life, as well as the results of sowing and planting at the waxing of the moon. Lakhovsky succeeded, by the simple expedient of using an open copper circuit to surround the plant, in curing mortal plant disease, and in producing prolific growth. The circuit absorbed an extra supply of cosmic rays. A copper girdle along these lines was also found greatly to benefit human health.

The psychological effect of the full moon has been fully recognised of late by the medical profession. But it has always been a big factor in the lives of simple intuitive people such as savages, and even in highly cultured ancient races. In fact, many of the recent 'discoveries' mentioned in this chapter are not new at all. Colour, perfume and sound were always fully utilised by the intelligentsia of ancient times—the priesthood. The chanting, incense and priestly vestments of most temples and churches bear witness to this. Such practices brought radiation into use for the production of desired psychological effects.

Plato was said to have studied the ancient cults of perfume and colour with Solon, who had access to the Egyptian archives.

Among some of the Zuni Indian tribes of New Mexico an ancient practice still exists. This is to take certain large sea-shells, reduce their surface to extreme thinness, and paint them with the seven colours of the spectrum. The shell is then held between the ear and the sun, and said to produce musical notes which can effect healing. Pythagoras himself evolved the term 'chromatic scale' because he believed that musical notes were coloured, or allocated to colours.

The medicine men of many ancient tribes use colours in various ways, either painting the affected parts of their patients with them or exciting them with coloured masks and chantings. Certain of the old races were said to regulate conception by the phases of the moon. All of them took the moon into account in their agricultural activities.

If we consider the animal kingdom in relation to the world of radiations we may well believe what Lakhovsky says with regard to the instincts of animals and insects and birds. He suggests that all these instincts are actual functions corres-ponding to sight and hearing, but that they operate upon the medium of the subtle rays which we have been discussing. He says that animals and insects tune in to the rays of the thing they are seeking, be it food or mate. He suggests that the antennae of insects and the tails of animals perform the function of wireless receivers, and that birds become so highly electrically charged while flying through the air that they can tune in to very far distances, as in migration. This theory, which is said to have been already proven through experi-ment, certainly explains much which was quite inexplicable before.

We therefore see the wonderful world of hidden energies being gradually discovered and unfolded before us. This latest realm of research is doing more to explain to us the forces which build up the fabric and run the engine of life than did all preceding scientific efforts. Year by year the scientist gets nearer to copying the processes which produce living tissues. He can now take the milk from the cow, and, by a wonderful chemical procedure, produce imitation ivory and bone from it, which is extraordinarily like the real thing. To do this he copies the processes to which milk is subjected within the body of the growing calf, such as heat, pressure and the action of substances such as formic acid. The scientist can also copy the work of the silkworm, producing beautiful artificial silk through the blending of very much the same materials as the silkworm uses. These are cellulose and alkali and acid substances, combined through the action of heat or radiant energy. He has also succeeded in imitating the wool of the sheep to such a degree that he is likely to spoil the wool markets! In his laboratories he has been able to persuade living tissue to continue growing, away from its parent body. His very latest achievement is to produce baby rabbits from a virgin mother without, apparently, using a male rabbit in any way.

There seems to be no end to what the modern scientist can do. The complete conquest of matter which he is so quickly achieving should make us pause to wonder what the next cycles of human endeavour can possibly have in store for us. All the latest inventions have been in the realm of the invisible, bringing into subjection and use rays and energies of ever-diminishing wave-length and subtler potency. The electrical kingdom, of which we have been speaking in this chapter, covers a very wide area indeed. Electricity, heat, light, magnetism, force and radiation are closely bound together. When we remember that the particles of an atom of the heaviest, most solid substance are composed of electric charges it becomes clear that it is impossible to draw the line between electricity (or force) and matter.

The point that appears to be forgotten is that when a

mineral particle is discharged into the air from its parent atom, and is then spoken of as a particle of electricity, it does not necessarily *lose its mineral character.* The electrons in an atom of iron, for instance, would seem, as we before concluded, to be each of a different mineral character, in keeping with the larger atom—the solar system. Why should they lose their *individual* character upon escaping from the atom, even although their electrical nature becomes thus more evident? Minerals and metals have a solid state and also a liquid state. What about their gaseous state? *How much difference may there really be between electricity and travelling particles of gaseous mineral?*

The spectroscope reveals that chemicals and metals are found in the sun's composition and rays. Experiments carried out in the stratosphere have shown that the sun's rays penetrate to the earth without appreciable loss of their constituents. These constituents include metals and chemicals in gaseous form, a tremendous range of rays, including infra-red and ultra-violet, besides ions and electrons, and many less definable energies. When these rays are reflected by the moon on to the earth they are modified by the moon's particular mineral content, the sum of which would make up the moon's frequency and wave-length. But after modification they are reflected, nevertheless, being extremely powerful although wielding a different influence from when they left the sun.

In the same way the sun's rays are reflected outward again by each of the planets. Every one of these, being different in the sum of their mineral make-up, wave-length and frequency, reflect back a different modification of the sun's rays. As the planets are much more powerful and larger than our little moon, the rays which we receive from them must necessarily be relatively more important. But outside our solar system there are stars and suns of a magnitude which almost passes our imagination. The great sun Sirius, for

instance, and the colossal globe of Aldebaran, must be sending out rays compared with which our solar system and its
radiations are but a speck of dust floating upon their giant
beams! What can be the influence and effect of those vast
forces, so far quite outside our scientific ken, which cross and
criss-cross and reflect and vibrate, producing one vast ocean
of rays pouring out in every direction? In the midst of this
pulsating life the stars and constellations are poised, beating
and oscillating centres of energy, held in place and in action
by some force which stands in inscrutable strength and
silence before the awakening gaze of material science.

23

The Kingdom of Mind

Having risen to splendid heights of achievement, the modern scientist, if he be of a materialistic type, might feel inclined to use his successes to disprove religion or the existence of a spiritual world.

'I can show you how everything is made,' he would say. 'In my laboratory I can copy everything in nature. I can show you exactly how a solar system comes into being—I can even put the constituents together in miniature myself, and set it going by rotation! It's not necessary to bring a Deity into this—it's all quite straightforward and merely due to chemical reactions!'

He forgets that in this case *he* is acting the part of the miniature Deity who is putting a miniature solar system into action! He forgets that his mind, his inventiveness, his actions and his determination have all to be there *before* anything can happen in his laboratory.

Material science can explain a very great deal about life as it exists. It can even explain how its later phases came into existence. It can describe and correctly estimate so many of the laws of nature, and the reactions of one thing upon another. But it does not attempt to explain where the ideas, the plans, the calculations, the millions of marvellous designs and shapes came from. Although it is known that man uses his mind to produce ideas, designs and plans, and although it is known that ideas, designs and plans were already being put in action in nature long before men's minds were functioning as minds at all, yet the materialistic scientist dare not postulate the obvious inference—that there is and has been, since the dawn of life, some Great Mind at work. This must be a Mind built on such tremendous lines that it has been able to take a long-distance view of constellations, and plan the vast cycles of the Greater Zodiac; yet it must also possess capacities sufficiently finite to design the fabric of an atom, and imbue each electrical particle with the genius of heredity. This Mind appears to be initiating all processes, flowing like invisible life-blood throughout the universe, and finding its reflection only in the finite mind of man himself.

As we are discussing the findings of modern science in this portion of our work, we may not at present look back into the past for the opinions of the ancient scientists upon the subject of the mind. We must confine ourselves to the work that has been done during the last few generations, since the present 'age of science' began to take an interest in human psychology.

It is many years now since the cry 'mind over matter' was first heard. The realisation that the power of the human mind could radically influence the cells of the body, effecting profound changes in them, and revolutionising the state of health, was the result of various demonstrations. The work of Mesmer, for instance, did much to open people's eyes to the extraordinary mystery of the mind, its hidden reaches and its untold possibilities. Hypnotism still further emphasised the fact that the mind, when divorced from waking consciousness, is far more powerful than when allied with waking consciousness; that it has the capacity deliberately to travel to any distance and record facts; that it can tap knowledge entirely outside its normal control; and that it can influence the body to act or to develop in ways quite impossible to it in the waking state.

The demonstrations of Christian Scientists and the work

of Dr. Coué brought these discoveries to a further stage, by showing that it was possible for the mind to produce radical effects upon human conditions while in the *waking* conscious state. Nobody seemed to give any clear explanation of these phenomena. The words 'faith' and 'science' were somewhat confusedly interchanged.

Meanwhile a body of thought which strictly tabooed the 'spiritual' aspect of the question was growing to proportions where it began to claim the public attention. This was built up by the psycho-analysts. These men, working entirely from the materialistic standpoint, with enormous patience, accumulated an amount of somewhat confusing evidence about the processes of the human psyche and their effect upon health and metabolism. To begin with they left the human soul out of the picture altogether. They even tried to ignore the genius of the human abstract mind. They considered man rather more as an animal, which, in fact, he is when the two higher factors of his nature mentioned above are ruled out.

Taking the Darwin theory as their starting-off point, the early psychologists of last century studied the physical reflexes of the human and animal body, the memory patterns, the habit patterns, and the 'instincts' which men share with the animals. They took a step further when they stated that the brain and the mind were one, and later when they identified the mind with the whole nervous system. Finally they discovered that the mind was present in every tissue of the body.

One of the most important centres of this early work was the School of Nancy, which after lengthy experiments declared that the body was controlled by the mind, the mind could be controlled by suggestion, and that suggestion was made effectual by hypnotism.

Suggestion later gave place in favour of auto-suggestion. By this method the patient, instead of mechanically obeying the expressed will of the hypnotiser, was induced to impress certain wishes and commands upon his own consciousness by his own 'super-conscious mind'. It was found that important results could be achieved if this work were carried out when the patient was in a passive state, preferably just before falling asleep.

Through hypnotism and suggestion it was gradually discovered that a tremendous storage of memories and impressions lies beneath the threshold of waking consciousness. This enormous complex content was named either the 'psyche' or the subconscious. The method of analysing its activities came to be known as psycho-analysis. This analysing process was carried out by searching and persistently questioning the patient, rooting out his most private memories and feelings, and forcing his mind back over many practically forgotten incidents of his earliest years. The method was at first somewhat brutal and extremely painful to the susceptibilities of highly-strung patients. But soon the most distressing conditions had been cured by these means, and although the practitioners made mistakes, and were confused by the wealth of puzzling material which they rapidly collected, it was evident that psycho-analysis had come to stay.

This science suffered, of course, in its infancy, not only from inexperience but from the overworking of certain of its aspects by people inclined to have one-track minds. In other words, it suffered from the prevailing sin of separatism. For instance, Professor Sigmund Freud, who established a school in Vienna, discovered the variety of psychological and pathological effects which sexual repressions may produce. This theme was run to death, almost every aspect of human life being put under the heading of sex of a rather animal type. In this way the public was caused to conceive a disgust for the new science of psycho-analysis. If only it could have been recognised that the physical sex instinct is a facet of the spiritual creative instinct, and some enlightenment upon the subject could have been obtained from the Ageless Wisdom, time would have been saved.

Some useful work was done by such men as Pfister, who evolved the theory that the impressions of early childhood controlled all later developments. From there began the study of the effect of childhood impressions upon the glands. The profoundly detrimental action upon metabolism of repressions, inhibitions, uncongenial associations, jealousy and lack of creative work was gradually brought to light. It was found that dyspepsia was often due to worry, appendicitis could be brought on by a long quarrel, perversion by unsatisfactory parental relationships, hysteria and paralysis through repression of a fright or shock in childhood, sexuality by lack of suitable creative employment, and various peculiar habits or traits by shyness, inhibitions and misunderstanding during adolescence. By exposing these hidden psychological knots to the light of day and the scrutiny of common sense a cure was often effected.

Any abnormal psychological condition such as those cited above, as well as tendencies to lie, steal, deceive, or even various types of insanity, were all found in the last analysis to be intimately connected with irregularities, deficiencies, or abnormalities of the endocrine glands. It could therefore be stated that the mind dwelt almost as intimately within these glands as it did within the brain. But the psycho-analysts are inclined to put everything down to repressions. The glandular experts concentrate entirely upon the glands. The biochemists can think of nothing but cell-salts. The radiologists believe that artificial oscillations can put the whole world right. Were these sciences only able to synthesise instead of separate themselves we should see an all-round method of healing of extreme value come into existence.

Dr. Alfred Adler, of Vienna, added valuable contributions to the psycho-analytical work which was being extensively conducted. He was interested in particular in what he called the 'psychic compensation of inferior organs'. He studied the vast array of mental and physical disabilities which spring up as the result of inferiority of the various organs. This is usually of ante-natal or hereditary origin. We know now that a deficiency in any of the principal organs of the body is intimately connected with its neighbouring endocrine gland, and is really due to imperfect glandular secretion. We know also that the particular cells producing such secretion are depending upon the correct flow of cosmic radiations through their circuits. So the final question is, of course, 'What is the influencing factor which regulates, inhibits or disturbs the flow of these cosmic radiations through the glands and organs?' The only force which could affect radiations would be radiations themselves, stronger or emanating from a source in the immediate vicinity. This source of radiations in immediate proximity to the glands in question is *the mind*!

To return to Dr. Adler. He declared that any organ which was inferior in development received the particular attention of the psyche. This means that a person who had a stutter, for instance, would be inclined to build up his whole character around his defective organ, always having his attention subconsciously fixed upon his throat and speech. In a person of weak character this would result in accentuated shyness and incoherency. But in an intellectual and vital person the result would be that his higher faculties would be drawn into expression through the medium of the deficiency, in a sub-conscious effort at compensation; he would then develop into a successful orator, actor or singer. His defect would serve only as added piquant attraction to his personality.

This is what Adler calls compensation for organ inferiority. He cites cases such as the defective ears of Mozart, the otosclerosis of Beethoven, and the aural hallucinations of Schumann in support of his theory. Many other examples will come to mind. The author has known both artists and surgeons who enjoyed the use of only one eye, and several other cases where disability has apparently proved to be a great incentive. History contains many illustrations of this, in the extremely difficult physical liabilities endured by certain famous men. In these cases it is apparent that the discomfort of the affliction in question rouses the mind to exert its power and produce such compensation as it can. This is usually translated into activity in its own realm—that of thought.

In this connection it is interesting to note that inferiority in the sex organs leads, in many cases, first of all to the attention being directed thereto, resulting in sex excesses or perversions or other abnormalities; secondly, in a vital person, the upper creative instincts and the upper glands strive to 'compensate', producing remarkable achievement. We therefore may have the spectacle, so strange and yet so usual, of a person of gifts or of genius producing creative work of lofty and spiritual inspiration, while in his personal life he persistently commits excesses in direct contradiction to his own expressed ideals. If we refer back to the chapters on Initiation and the Rays we shall be able to identify such cases quite easily. Here we actually see the battle going on between the soul and the personality, the higher and the lower bodies, associated with the Fourth Ray of 'Harmony through Conflict'.

The practice of psycho-analysis soon became more and more involved. The practitioners, as they became expert, found themselves rooting out all kinds of unknown symbols and designs from the subconscious strata of their patients' minds, which seemed to have profound psychological effects upon them. Many of these symbols had been unknown to the patients in their ordinary lives. After much inquiry it was discovered that some of them were ancient, long-forgotten religious or tribal symbols, dated many thousands of years ago. Some of the patients, while under suggestion, drew and coloured original and sometimes complicated geometrical designs, which seemed to give them great relief from their neurosis or inhibition. Such designs are called Mandalas, and their production is an ancient practice.

The psycho-analysts and psychologists were now faced with facts before which they could no longer treat the human being as an animal with extra brain powers. They were finally obliged to search about for more subtle explanations of the phenomena they were unearthing. One of their most enterprising members, Dr. C. G. Jung, then turned to the East for an explanation of some of the atavistic mystical concepts which came to light from the subconscious of most unexpected and prosaic people.

It was realised little by little that the response of the patient to these various symbols, which were definitely mystical or metaphysical in origin, and which were buried in the furthest depths of the 'sub-conscious', was sometimes more profound than his response to the incidents and situations which had conditioned his outer life. It was gradually brought to light that pre-natal inheritance did *not* account for much that lies buried in the human mind. Nor did the theories of the early psychologists with regard to automatic reflexes and memory habits account for the many strange phenomena which were demonstrated by such people as the spiritualists and the hypnotists. Hypnotic trance and mediumistic trance produced at times the most unaccountable results. There occurred cases when the subject spoke fluently in dead or unknown languages, or gave information about conditions and events in ancient civilizations which in the ordinary way he could have had no means of contacting. Eastern philosophy and religious thought began to flow through the mouths of uneducated and simple trance-mediums. It was clear that Eastern thought was invading the West, in spite of the fact that it was largely mistrusted, misunderstood and misused. Eastern thought was invading the West because there was a certain part of the human mind or psyche which was in some way allied to it. This part of the human make-up was evidently extremely important, and had not as yet been located or taken into account by the psycho-analysts.

This confusion had, of course, come about because of separatism. It was not considered the thing for material science, even when dealing with the reflexes of the human soul, to take its existence into account. Presumably some at least of the hard-working body of psychologists and psycho-analysts were devoutly religious men and sincere Christians, whose faith was founded upon the existence of the soul. Yet they dare not take it into consideration in their work. It was 'not the thing' even for a doctor to take the soul into his diagnosis, or to mention the soul to the most devout of his patients, even if they were quite obviously suffering from soul-starvation or soul-deficiency!

Separatism ruled the day.

Therefore, in taking one of the first steps to destroy this ridiculous state of affairs Dr. Jung performed a mighty service. He stepped right out of orthodoxy and began earnestly to search into the psychology of the soul. To do this he had to apply to the only people who had ever made a profound study of it—the Easterns. The result was that, in company with Richard Wilhelm, he published a book called *The Secret of the Golden Flower*. In this book ancient Chinese metaphysical science was interpreted and translated into terms of modern psychological science. The two met and agreed completely, the Eastern carrying on exactly from where the Western came to a pause. The Eastern doctrine gives an explanation of the correct development and growth of the soul, its reflexes and reactions to physical life. It seeks to avoid the complexities which are the result of succeeding stages of growth, or the terrible complications which occur if soul-growth is thwarted.

Dr. Jung's book explains the ancient science of Meditation from the psychological point of view. Our own brief résumé of this subject (see *The Finding of the Third Eye*) should be referred to as well. It will then become clear that the full process of meditation, including preliminary self-examination, nightly review, and the practices of concentration, meditation and contemplation, performed in conjunction with slow breathing, complete a system of psychological curative training which should be the envy of every physician and psychologist. The preliminary self-examination is an act of auto-psycho-analysis. The nightly review prevents the reforming of new inhibitions and repressions, and ensures good sleep. Concentration produces a state of permanent self-control. Meditation eliminates superficial worrying and thinking, in favour of an expansion of the whole mental attitude. Contemplation encourages that inspiration to flow in which is every man's birthright. Besides this the Eastern methods, which are not, of course, confined to the Chinese, encourage the students to reach out without fear to contact the Great Mind which is the designer of this universe.

A method of training based slightly along these lines, and adapted to the Western mentality, has been evolved under the name of Pelmanism, the great success of which testifies to the soundness of its psychology. It should be an encouraging thought that so many people are becoming ready to take their personal training and development into their own hands. In this way some of the unfortunate results of mass education are being overcome.

It will naturally take time for Jung's pregnant message to penetrate and take effect where it is most needed. But the seeds have been sown, and fortunately Dr. Jung has fellow pioneers who are putting his findings into practice, or else working on similar lines. Dr. Robert Assagioli has a scientific institution in Florence, the Institute of Psychosynthesis, and sets out deliberately to psycho-analyse that part of the human psyche which we know as the soul.[1] He puts down many human ills to the thwarting of soul development. He seeks to give people a fuller and deeper understanding of the conflicts going on within them, and of the glorious unfoldment which is striving to take place. This is a great improvement upon the old form of psycho-analysis, which presented man to himself as a complex mass of reflexes and cravings mostly of an unpleasant nature, and sometimes produced deeper revulsions than those which it cured.

The ingredients of any healing method should contain some instructions calculated to fill the patient with hope, inspiration, a feeling that life is purposeful and worth while under any conditions. Such ideas are fully and adequately put forward in the Ageless Wisdom. They are to be found in most great religions when correctly interpreted. Having acknowledged the power of mind over matter, and having proved its workings scientifically, it seems reasonable to suggest that the healing professions use those mind-incentives and mind-healers provided by sound metaphysical instruction. The deterrent to such logical procedure seems to be that so many of the professions are themselves the victims of the inhibitions and repressions which they are seeking in various ways to cure.

Why should not a physician be able to recommend to his patients certain books to read, calculated to help him in his particular need?

Why should a physician not be able to send certain of his patients to church? Why should not a physician use psychological knowledge effectively, and be competent to send a patient to the particular church where he knew a certain kind of sermon would be given by a priest of such a type that the whole would tune in to the patient's need? Why should not the priest in his turn study psychology, the psychology particularly of certain of his congregation, in company with

[1] See his new book *Psychosynsthesis* (pub: 1968).

their physicians, and by mutual arrangement ensure the preaching of certain effective sermons at stated times? These would seem to be the most obvious and simple collaborative methods to any not badly infected with the disease of separatism. When the results of separatism upon human life can clearly be faced by men who have expunged it from their own systems it will be seen to be a mental disease, producing dire results.

But we are not as far as that yet. Only when the science of the soul has been brought forward by physicians as a paramount factor in healing will the barriers separating the two in the human mind-habits be broken down. Only when the radical effects which emotions, ideals, worries and grudges exert upon the human metabolism have been publicly and exhaustively demonstrated will the public allow doctors to escape from the rut of treating them by medicine alone. The best method of such demonstration is undoubtedly through the films. Here again separatism must be overcome; the film experts must be encouraged to work with doctor and scientist and educationalist. It must be made worth their while to produce the enormous array of thrillingly fascinating instructive films which are awaiting their inspiration.

For the health question, especially from the psychological side, is inevitably reduced in its final analysis to the question of education. Education must be planned by scientist, metaphysician, physician and priest working together, and becoming so thoroughly conversant with each other's angles of study that in time the differences between them are completely fused.

24

Fusion

W E have now completed our brief outline of both material and spiritual science. Behind the slight indications which we have given there lies an inexhaustible wealth of material in each realm. In these chapters, however, a specific attempt has been made to pick out certain highlights illustrating the point of our argument. This argument declares that there is a fundamental synthesis and unity of all aspects of life. It stresses the existence of a vital spiritual world, and the importance of the material scientist's physical world, declaring both to be integrated facets of one whole.

Those readers who are interested in this issue will have been able to pick out various striking examples of this integration as we went along. It now remains for us to press the point home by summing up a few of the clearest examples.

Before one can prove that a theory is true there has to exist the theory to be proved. The theory in this case is stated by the Ageless Wisdom, and is the postulate of World Initiation. This has been worked out and compiled so very much more fully than I have been able to indicate in these few pages. A theory can be proven through individual personal experience, which in the case of the Wisdom has been attested to by many hundreds of redoubtable and important figures in history. Or it can be proven to suit the public *en masse,* and to satisfy other types of minds, by concrete 'orthodox' science. This latter proof is being brought forward in increasing measure today.

The practical materially-minded scientist of the present time is doing a greater service to spiritual thought than perhaps any other section of thinkers. He is responding to the need of the awakening attention of humanity upon the mental plane. The Wisdom is coming into the light of day once more. The Church stands firm and steady. But neither is complete without a proper fusion with the practical everyday working world. This fusion and interpretation is being brought about by the scientist. Step by step he is proving and working out and making public every statement of importance contained in the Ancient Wisdom. When a sufficient number of these statements have been shown to be scientifically correct it will begin to be possible to conceive that the rest of the Wisdom is also true. When considered squarely in this light it will be found that the Wisdom provides the forgotten answers to many of the puzzling veiled phrases in the Old and New Testaments, and supplies new beauty, strength and certainty to the Christian faith. It will be found also that it provides unending leaders and pointers to the scientist, indicating to him what lies ahead in the realm of discoveries, and where and how to look for it.

The scientists are doing such intensive, rapid and amazing work nowadays that they are speeding up spiritual progress in a way which becomes thrilling to the intuitive observer. For at this present stage, which we dealt with in the chapter on Initiation, spiritual progress depends upon the development of concentration in, and a shift of focus into, the mental plane; first the plane of concrete mind, and then the plane of higher dynamic thought. It has to be learnt that physical, chemical, scientific, practical and spiritual activities and aspects of life are all one and identical with the Divine. Man, through his own mental activity, is to learn to *know* his God, so that he no longer needs to *believe* in Him. Thus will knowledge and increasing creative powers draw him ever nearer to the final mystery—complete *identification* with God Himself.

This statement, which men are so rapidly demonstrating, is one of the prominent pronouncements in the Wisdom itself.

A further statement is that matter and spirit are one.

Scientists state that matter in its last analysis is energy. The ultimate atom is composed of energy in varying rates of oscillation.

The Wisdom declares that all life is formed on a system of delicately graded states of matter, called 'planes', of finer and finer atoms.

Science is proving that the finest particles of physical matter have already led us through into the electrical kingdom, and that still finer divisions in the electrical kingdom produce the wave-lengths of thought, leading us through into the realm of mind. It has proved that these thought radiations show actual spectral colours, and have sufficient physical potency to move metal instruments. It has proved that a lump of sugar can be rapidly transmuted in the human system into a thought of love or hate, and that the only 'physical' change has been in rate of vibration. Scientists are gradually ascending the long ladder of vibrations, conquering and discovering ever finer, subtler, shorter wave-lengths. This long ladder is nothing less than the famous Jacob's Ladder, leading from earth to heaven.

The Wisdom declares this present phase of physical life to be planned upon the number seven.

Science agrees that the spectrum of colours, the musical scale, the atomic weights and corresponding character of atoms, the periods in lunar influence, affecting agriculture, health and disease in animal, insect and germ, and various other phenomena, are largely based upon the octave of seven.

The Wisdom declares man to be a copy in miniature of greater existences in the universe, and built upon a system of seven major 'centres', or vortices through which the essences of life are fed to him. These vortices have, since earliest

Egyptian times, been allocated to the positions held by the seven major endocrine glands.

Scientists are deeply engaged with the study of the importance of the glands, and the fact that they are being fed by the cosmic rays, which contain subtle metallic and mineral particles.

The alchemits of the Wisdom declare that the elixir of life, the ultimate essence which produces health and growth and progress in man, is formed of the essence or spirit of metals; and that the medicine *par excellence* will be found when men can transmute and set free that essence for themselves.

The Wisdom embraced scientific astrology as another of its branches, declaring that the stars rule and control physical manifestation, and that the trends both in individual and collective life can be ascertained by a study of them.

Science has arrived at the point where the colossal influence exercised most intimately upon life by rays coming from outside the solar system has become clear.

Astrology further declares that a forecast of an existence can be made from a study of the cosmic influences playing upon it at the time of birth.

Modern science has proved that the character and growth of a plant is radically altered according to the lunar and stellar and solar phases under which it is planted. So it appears that even this most disputed branch of spiritual lore is soon to be proven or explained by practical science.

The Wisdom encouraged the practice of self-culture by means of diet, breathing, relaxation and meditation. These sciences were thoroughly worked out, and are best known under the Indian systems of Yoga, although they exist in other countries as well.

Science advocates and studies these practices of self-culture also. Now that humanity is emerging from the Dark Age the cry on all sides is for health-culture and mind-culture. The interest in health, sport, diet, psychology—and finally the 'occult' sciences—all testify to the rebirth of 'Yoga' under a modern guise.

The Wisdom states that the later development of man will be from selfish self-consciousness to co-operative group consciousness, and from nationalism to internationalism.

On all sides we see the violent signs of struggle going on as these newer qualities are being brought to birth, in the teeth of tremendous opposition from the older forces. These interesting factors, so plainly at work in the world, need not here be enlarged upon. They only need looking for to be seen!

The Wisdom postulates the spiral cyclic development of life, and the evolution of the various kingdoms throughout definite periods of time, each of a stipulated character and influence.

Modern history and archaeology are rapidly enlarging their scope of vision to the point where these great periods begin to be dimly visible and recognisable. There are those already who are endeavouring to work out periods for us, showing how they have manifested in history.

The wisdom declares that the sun is literally the heart of the solar system, which latter is one great Entity. Its life-blood, which is not so chemically solid as ours, although containing the same ingredients, circulates throughout all Its organs (the planets), nourishing the entire organism. The Entity breathes as we do, the great breaths passing through the heart (sun), the full expiration taking place every eleven years.

Science has now discovered that the atmosphere is packed with different subtle ingredients, including, in a fine form, all the elements which make up the earth. It states also that the sun has periodical phases distinguished by the appearance and activity of sun-spots, which reach their maximum in numbers and in outpouring every eleven years. These sun-spots are described as vast craters from which an extra flow of gases and energies rushes forth. It has been shown that the periods of minimum or maximum sun-spots have a potent effect upon weather and climatic conditions, upon the growth and flavour of the plant world, upon the nervous and emotional condition of men and animals, and upon all work which is being done with electro-magnetic waves.

Sir William Herschel has decided that 'a scarcity of vegetation occurs whenever the sun appears to be free from spots'. Moreux observed that the yield of wheat throughout the world followed these variations of solar activity. He also deduced from psychological observations that solar activity powerfully affected human nervous excitability, and said that 'a relation could conceivably exist between wars and the sun'. Experiments have shown that the best vintage years correspond exactly with a maximum of activity in sun-spots. Dr. Fauré and Dr. Sardou have observed that the number of cases of sudden death corresponds closely with the height of solar energy. Sir James Jeans has remarked that a study of the cross-sections of trees shows that the thickest rings were formed every eleven years at the time of maximum sun-spots. Dr. Conyers Morrell and other doctors have observed that waves of epidemic disease correspond closely with the times of minimum sun-spot activity. A large number of other phenomena and conditions are being associated with the phases of the sun's activity. This year itself, 1939,[1] marks one of the eleven-year peaks of sun-spot activity. We shall be able to watch its influence in the heightened human tension everywhere, in corresponding storms and electrical disturbances and a generous yield of the fruits of the earth.[2]

It would be possible to continue indefinitely these analogies between Ageless Wisdom and modern science. If any further interesting examples occur to my readers I should be glad to

[1] This also applies to 1947 (Author 1947).
[2] This was so! (Author 1943).

hear from them. Enough has already been said, however, to prove that the original exponents of the Ageless Wisdom had access to real knowledge, and a largeness of vision which applied that knowledge to bigger issues than our modern scientists yet do. The Ageless Wisdom set before us the whole panorama of evolving life, presenting it from the fundamental aspects of cause and purpose. The cause was Deity, and the purpose was a fresh impulse of growth in the creative aspect of Deity. The result is said to be that each human being is gradually evolving into a potential Deity, with a future before him of glory and interest inexpressible.

The Ageless Wisdom sets out the whole picture before us definitely and clearly, exposing to us a future, a goal, a plan and a method, into whose pattern everything we know and experience slips as into a Chinese puzzle. If we accept this exposition the whole of life is completely altered for us, and our own rapid expansion becomes possible and inevitable. At first that which the Wisdom states seems utterly impossible and incomprehensible. But in measure as we awaken the dormant brain-cells relative to those ideas, so do those ideas become logical, practical and acceptable to us.

The Ageless Wisdom presents the plan of life to us from its highest, vastest, most intangible aspects, down to the last detail in scientific chemical analysis. True, it is often given in veiled and symbolic language, but not more veiled to the layman than are the technical and Latin terms of modern science. If it be found that the Wisdom has dealt competently with the scientific facts which scientists are laboriously bringing to light one by one, surely it is logical to assume that those facts stated by the Wisdom which the scientist has not yet uncovered are also likely to be true?

Let us consider what are the principal and most significant statements of the Wisdom which are not yet possible of any orthodox scientific proof whatsoever. This will bring us right into the heart of the subject of these chapters, that of World Initiation and the evolution which the whole of life is undergoing. These teachings try to shake man out of his habit of considering his minute self as the one and only type of being capable of self-conscious existence and individual creative thought. They try to make him realise that he is an existence in the midst of a long scale of other existences of myriad kinds, and that he must transcend the limitations imposed by his size by using that part of him which is not limited by physical form. He is asked to visualise the Path of Initiation, which marks for all life the stages of evolution. He is required to understand the entifying of every aspect of life by entities who are part of one great consciousness. He is asked to learn to grasp how the many can exist as the One without loss of identity. He is instructed to believe in a glorious consummation which awaits all life travelling along the Path of Initiation.

Let us consider how near orthodox science has come to an elucidation of any of these concepts. It has discovered, as we have seen, that the entire universe is *one* in its radiatory and mineral interactions—that it is a great organism in which no divisions can be made. The processes of reflection and radiation are repeated and re-repeated unendingly between and through sun, moon and planets until it is impossible to allocate any one ray entirely to any one source or sources. Furthermore, we have learnt that we are fundamentally affected and influenced at the very cores of our cells by the life of other planets. We know that the other planets contain many of the same ingredients as our own, and that those which they do not contain are radiated to them one from another. The difference in planets is due to temperature and rate of vibration. But, as we know that *conscious* life—that is to say thought and feeling—exists in high vibrational rates we cannot reasonably say that no conscious life exists on the other planets.

We are therefore already making the first approach to the concept of the one great physical and self-conscious Life, containing lesser ones within it. If we can get used to the idea of considering our own planet as a living Being, the sum of our consciousness, we will gradually be able to think of any star as a being, a 'person', and of the firmament as a crowd of people, the sum of whose consciousness is the mind of a greater Entity. That these 'people' are vast deities compared with ourselves is an overwhelming truth, which is only offset by the fact that we are capable of conceiving of them and thinking about them.

Let us see how near science is coming to the subject of initiation and transmutation. It has already discovered that the earth and the solar system as a whole is steadily becoming lighter in weight, and more ethereal in physical character, by reason of the continuous splitting up of the grosser atoms and the radiation of their particles. This process, of course, includes every living thing upon the earth.

Science is giving up the idea of considering volcanoes, storms, winds and other intense expressions of the elements as due to chance, and involuntary and accidental sequences of effects. It is now busy looking for astrological explanations of these phenomena. Science has placed its· hands upon the heart-beat of the sun and its fingers upon the pulse of the life-blood of the solar system. It is psycho-analysing the solar mind in every effort it makes to understand the workings of nature. It is approaching thrillingly near to a blinding realisation of the great Entity himself. When this happens— and nothing can stop it—man's little mind will have tuned finally, by his own efforts, up to the tempo of the greater Mind. Like a tiny bubble of quicksilver his understanding will rush to join the greater understanding, and the ultimate fusion will have taken place.

25

How to Co-operate

To the reader who has found himself stimulated by the ideas brought forward in this book there will doubtless occur two questions.

He will first be inclined to ask what the result would be in human affairs of a general acceptance of the Ageless Wisdom. Being, as most intelligent people really are, practically-minded, he will want to know in what way its doctrines, especially the one of World Initiation as emphasised in these pages, could be of definite usefulness to people at this time.

If he is convinced that the Ageless Wisdom can supply the explanations and inspirations needed for the betterment of world affairs as a whole, his next question will be : How best can a person who accepts these doctrines, and wishes to march with the vanguard of humanity, co-operate, in his life and habits, with the ideals set forth? What are the principal ways in which he might be of service, irrespective of his work or position in life?

In these closing pages we will endeavour to answer as well as we may these two questions.

Possibly this is the first time the subject of World Initiation has been so directly put forward before the general reader. Doubtless it will outrage certain susceptibilities. Those susceptibilities will have been nourished on inhibitions, inhibitions which may have been proper and right a few generations ago, but which will soon have to give way to the changing times. Doubtless also these doctrines will strike a deep chord in many inquiring minds, and awaken the response of instinctive recognition. But were these ideas and ideals to be taken up as a new general standard of thought by a responsible section of the public the results would certainly be epoch-making. If people were to accept the fact of individual continual progress throughout many lives, for every living creature; if they were to realise that world-wide integrated brotherhood was a scientific fact, and begin to consider themselves always in relation to the planetary Being; if they could understand that they can no more evade the Path of Initiation and their ultimate birthright of perfection than they can evade death; if they could be made to glimpse a vision of the joy, the power, the knowledge and the experience that will be theirs when they learn to forsake their present prisons of ignorant, blind self-indulgence, and apply themselves to the pursuit of truth : if only an iota of all this could be absorbed by them as truth and not as theory, so that they began to fight their way out of the fogs and mists of stale and static thought-forms and to look at life with less biased eyes, then indeed the burdens of both weary humanity and the Hierarchy would be lightened, and patience and effort would be welcomed as the passports to new realms of glorious fruition.

International politics and economics, education and health would be revolutionised and planned from entirely new standpoints. Both nationally and individually the principal aims would be to avoid further Karma, to plan for the Path of Initiation and to learn to understand those factors in life which are fundamental. When once it became realised that no one man or nation could go forward while others were left behind, and that the ultimate attainment is achieved only when the slower or most imperfect member has caught up, then indeed would genuine co-operation and a sharing of supplies be the order of the day. Men have made widespread efforts all over the world for the stamping out of epidemics and disease because of the danger of their spreading to their own midst and the realisation of their harmfulness. In the same way, when ignorance and wrong-thinking are understood to be contagious and harmful diseases, spreading and infecting many through the medium of the ether and radiations, widespread and international efforts will readily be made to stamp them out also.

Some people hold back from the Wisdom because they consider it as belonging to the East. We have pointed out in these chapters that according to the Wisdom itself it came originally from the West, and, passing across to the north of Europe, was finally brought down first to India by the *white Aryan race* from which we spring! It was India's special mission to guard and hold it until the later Aryan sub-races should be ready for it. That is why we use the old Indian names for things of which we had no knowledge and for which we had no equivalent terms in our relatively young British tongue. We might perhaps have unearthed and used the Egyptian names instead, or the ancient Tibetan. But it is just that especial mixture of races in India which inclines the Westerns to assimilate ideas more easily from it.

The results of a belief in the Ageless Wisdom can really best be described by answering the second question, and indicating the way in which people will live who wish to co-operate with the Heirarchy. They will first of all bring their own lives into line with the teachings. The methods of so doing have already been described.[1] They will ensure the maximum of health, understanding and progress in the life of the individual. But self-development is only the first and rather elementary step upon the Path of Initiation. Actually the word 'self' is the same word as 'prison' when

[1] See *The Finding of the Third Eye*.

seen from intuitive levels. The aspirant must hope for the time when his methods of right living, right feeling and right thinking have become automatic and he can remove his attention safely from himself altogether. From that moment he can really become a helper of some account in the eyes of the Hierarchy, and work will be allocated to him by his invisible friends.

The aspirant must strive to become group-conscious instead of self-conscious, willing to sink his personality, his ambitions and his opinions, and work and share selflessly in group work. Later still he must become world-conscious as well as group-conscious—his group will then be the whole brotherhood of man. He must strive to shift his focus of vision from the particular to the universal, perceiving life in ever larger and broader terms. This does not mean that he shall cease to think of little daily matters as of any importance. On the contrary, he will see each one of them as a reflection of divine activities, and as affording practice for future achievements. In this light every little activity of daily life will take on an aspect of almost sacred and intense interest.

The aspirant will ever bear two key-words in his mind—synthesis and illumination. He will realise that progress comes through the breaking down of barriers and the abolishing of labels. He will understand that the rule of force and of separatism is over, and that love, toleration and gentleness can now win the day if only there is enough of it! He will shape his words and his influence to this belief. He may not be 'anti-' or 'pro-' any expression of life. He will simply understand the place of all parts within the whole. By his own living only may he show any propaganda. He will learn to trust in the influence of the radiations of his own clear, dynamic thinking. The power of silent thought will become as ready an instrument to his use as the power of speech.

The aspirant must become a psychologist. He must study his fellow men, clearly but uncritically, accepting them lovingly at their particular stage of unfoldment, but seeking to understand that stage so well that he is ready with the right word and the right thought when and if it is required of him. He can seek this understanding from whatever angle seems natural to him. This may be through a knowledge of the glands, the centres, the Rays, astrology or modern psychology. Whatever his approach, he must never forget its intrinsic synthesis with the other angles of approach.

The aspirant must give as creative a contribution as he is able to world progress. He must not rush forward determinedly and fanatically in order to 'do' something, or anything. He must watch and wait until his opportunity is made quite clear to him, ready to throw all his energy and intelligence into it when the indications are plain. But he must also remember that 'They also serve who only stand and wait'. Perhaps his work is to stand steady as an anchor, pouring out rays of truth to those who are in the thick of the fight. He must realise that in measure as he develops spiritually so will the problems which he has to decide and face become ever more subtle and difficult. But so also will spiritual radiance and realities become ever easier of access and ever simplifying towards the final unity.

In his psychological studies the aspirant must learn principally to be able to pick out those souls who are ready to go forward into the new age conditions and those who are not. This is really, of course, a question of initiations, and from that point of view is rather complex. We will look at it from an easier angle, making our division between those who are Aquarian in consciousness, or becoming so, and those who are still radically Piscean.

By Aquarians we mean those people, of any age, class or race, who, having passed through the lesser Aryan initiations, are gradually drawing near to the point when they will take the greater Aryan Initiation. This will pass them through into incarnation into the ranks of the forebears of the future Root-race. They will be the pioneers of the coming Golden Age. Their minds are already differently focused from the Piscean minds, and they are intuitively preparing for ways and conditions of life which will be quite different to anything we have known.

By Pisceans we mean those people, also of any age, class or race, who have not yet taken those lesser initiations which would expand their minds to an approach to future conditions. They are still enthralled and enclosed within the thought-walls of the Piscean Age, still completely tuned in to the mental outlook of the 'Age of Ignorance'. The Piscean Age, as you know, lasts two thousand or so years, as do the other Zodiacal Signs. Its inception marked the beginning of the Christian era. It is passing out of manifestation now, as the new Aquarian Age is coming in.

The typical Piscean is rather narrow and settled in his outlook. He may be a fine, intelligent character or the reverse. At his best he has a great love of his home, his family, his possessions, his country and his religion. Note that these things are all loved because they are *his*. The individual egoistic, possessive, *exclusive* attitude is his throughout. He *feels* strongly about things, rather than thinks. He is full of partisanship, prejudice and dogged opinions. He is anti-this and pro-that. He dislikes bringing his own mind to bear upon any new conception. The old ways are good enough for him. Especially is this so about religion. With the Christian religion, for instance, the Piscean is content in its simplest, most childish and unexplained form. He does not want to understand his religion. He wants to feel it, to be comforted, soothed and helped. In his prayers he always *asks* for those things he needs. He is as a child before his Maker. He is full of devotion to *his* relatives, to *his* God, to *his* work and achievement. If his emotions are touched he will give generously to any charity or need, but he does not want to bring thought to bear upon it if that can be avoided.

The Piscean, because he is still astrally focused, has a great love of beauty and art, luxury and comfort. Fundamentally his ideal life is to be surrounded with his personal comforts and family in a charming home, to have acquired importance in his profession, and not to be disturbed in any other way! He believes in war as a necessary evil. He is content to be preached to, talked at and dictated to in order not to think for himself.

The typical Aquarian has a viewpoint diametrically opposed to that of the Piscean. His outlook is broad and unsettled, quite open to change at any moment. He also may be a fine, intelligent character, or a wild irresponsible one. At his best he has a love of humanity without distinctions. He has a love of beauty, and of all the good qualities to be found everywhere in home life, in patriotism, in internationalism and in all religions. He is not possessive. All children seem to him to be his children, all parents his own. He cannot limit his love, his interest, his partisanship, his work, to any small personal circle. His answer to all ruts of thought, traditions, habits and fetishes is : 'Why?'

The Aquarian loves not with his emotions, but with his mind, that aspect of the *mind* which dwells in his heart. 'As a man *thinketh* in his heart, so is he.' His love comes through understanding, not feeling. He is therefore not swayed by emotion, and may be considered cold by the astrally poised. The true Aquarian shares. He shares his lives, his ideas, his work and his reward impersonally with others. He is group-centred instead of self-centred. He is inclusive instead of exclusive. He is unprejudiced and unopinionated, and 'anti' and 'pro' are not in his vocabulary.

The Aquarian likes to use his mind. He wants to know, through his *own* thinking, not somebody else's. He looks always to the future. He is very often a rebel, a spendthrift or a 'rolling stone'. But he is ready to work for the new ideas and to be drawn by the vibrations of the New Age, when he contacts them. He does not believe in war, he disapproves of force. He is not a slave to his comforts, his possessions or public opinion. His great ideal is to serve, but to serve all men rather than one or two.

In dealing with people, the aspirant cannot treat Aquarians and Pisceans alike. Unless he wishes to waste time, he need not present New Age ideas of life to the Piscean. The best he can do with a typical Piscean is to influence him to become a high-grade and good Piscean, and leave it at that. He can point out to him his need, if he is a Christian, to live up to a few of its fundamental principles; 'Love thy neighbour as thyself' is as good as any other! Let this include all nations, and let the Piscean begin quite simply to obey Christ's commands. He need do no more. It would be enough to change the world.

In dealing with the Aquarian, however, the approach must be quite different. For he has left spiritual childhood, and is becoming adult. He no longer asks for things in his prayers. He wants instead to give. He wants to help his Creator, to collaborate and co-operate with his plans, to show him some return for the riches of his gifts. He is ashamed of the emotional mess human beings have made of their lives. He wants to get busy and put things in order. Whether he is consciously religious or not, his practical attitude will be the same. He is ready to sink his individuality in the interest of the whole. He is forgetting himself. His view has broadened, and he finds life as a whole too interesting to become preoccupied with little troubles and petty gossips. He works towards synthesis, and towards the breaking down of barriers.

Future developments are always foreshadowed by the geniuses or gifted artists of the time. That this is so in the case of the coming Aquarian Age can quite clearly be seen.

In all creative art the tendency for some time has been to break established rules and traditions, escape from orthodoxy, rebel against classicism, and try out something new at all costs. 'Modern' music is an outstanding example of this, with its denial of established rhythms, its discords, its new subtleties and its cosmic feeling. Literature has reacted to the same influence, indulging in innovations which range all the way from crude 'realism' to complete meaninglessness, as, for example, in some of the efforts of James Joyce and Gertrude Stein. Art has performed outstanding propaganda on behalf of the new impending outlook. Impressionism, realism, surrealism, dada-ism, post-impressionism have followed one another in quick succession. They have shown forth the instinctive efforts to replace a highly developed sentimental photographic art, astral in its character, by a more abstract mental approach, in which the emotions and the physical realm are not the objective. In architecture we have seen perhaps the most remarkable revolution of all, due to the added influence upon it of changing modern life. The father of the arts has performed a complete *volte-face*, changing from the intricate, fussy, patterny ideas which embellished the end of the last century to the barest simplicity conceivable. This dignified plainness anticipated the renaissance of that metaphysical type of thought which distinguished great civilisations such as the early Egyptians when at the height of their spiritual culture, and later, in a more subtle form, the Greeks.

So, for those who can read the signs of the times, the coming psychological changes are being anticipated in the creative arts, and prepared for in other ways too. If we seek carefully for signs of the change of focus from the emotional into the mental we will find ourselves led, very surprisingly, to the University of Oxford. For, in spite of the many criticisms levelled at Oxford, there has been an undercurrent of psychological development taking place there which has per-

meated into the very life-blood of the nation. This development has masqueraded under the simple guise of a denial of
emotion! It has not been 'the thing' to feel emotion, and
entirely *infra dig.* to show it! This fetish has been the source
of much laughter and scorn, especially among the Latin
nations, but it has persisted nevertheless. By the end of last
century it had permeated into the English home, to the
extent that all topics engendering emotion, such as politics,
religion and health, were barred at the dinner-table. Even
the natural human appetites were denied, and it was correct
always to leave some food upon the plate! An extension of
this repression into the domain of love soon gave the English
a reputation for prudery and hypocrisy, which clings to them
to this day.[1]

Although its exterior phases were without charm, the
subjective significance of this development emanating from
Oxford was very deep. The denial of emotion and sentimen-
tality was the first step of emancipation from the thraldom
of the astral plane, a step that was being taken *collectively,*
in contrast to former individual spiritual development. As
England was the pioneer of this movement, this placed her
at the head of spiritual progress in a certain sense. The
esotericists have forecast an important future for England
in spiritual work. This means that the nation in some way
will lead other nations along the Initiatory Path.

There are two signs that this may be actually the case.
When an individual aspirant first shifts his consciousness
from the astral to the mental plane there ensures a phase of
disconnection in everyday life while adjustment to the new
rhythm is being acquired. This phase results in vagueness,
confusion and incompetence in outer living, which lasts
while the new inner links are being fused. England as a whole
is going through this phase at present. At the same time the
newer spiritual vision is filtering outwards. England has

[1] Not any more, 1968!—V.S.A.

latterly led the nations of Europe in standing for the newer Christianity, and in attempting, however falteringly, to be 'as wise as the serpent and as harmless as the dove'! And, naturally, in even stronger measure, will America, home of the future Race, subscribe to these ideals.

As the aspirant learns little by little to distinguish for himself these signs of the coming World Initiation he will be able to throw the weight of his approval, his thought, his encouragement and his co-operation behind all activities which he observes to be along progressive lines. All his words, actions and thoughts will tune in to the wave-lengths of progress, which he will recognise on all sides. He will encourage everyone towards synthesis, group-work and unity. He will foster always the larger outlook, the shifting of thoughts from the particular to the universal, the overcoming of personal emotionalism and touchiness and self-interest.

He will work for the development of 'Epigenisis'—individual creative thinking. He will endeavour to arouse people's minds to a realisation of the heavy smothering fogs of stale thought, habits and preconceptions which are blinding them to the light of truth. He will not act in a destructive or critical manner towards undesirable conditions, but will simply try to superimpose better ideas upon the old ones until they achieve a shifting of the attention from the old to the new.

He will make efforts to link up all those people one with another who are ready to fall in with the newer ideas and rhythms, and work for progress. He will make them known to one another, and strive for co-operation between their leaders. In all these efforts, which anyone can make from the centre of his own life and work, lies constructive help towards the consummation of the coming World Initiation, help towards humanity individually, and its Lord, the planetary being himself—whom men have called upon by the name of Adonai.

Finally, what shall the aspirant do for himself in order further to perfect himself as an instrument of service?

He must remember the purpose of all the information and ideas which are summarised in this book from the wealth of material available. That purpose is mind-expansion!—the vivifying of hitherto unused brain-cells and mind-cells. Knowledge in itself is only a key with which the door to life and truth is unlocked. Do not hug and prize the key and forget the door! The knowledge and study of the Wisdom are as the five-finger exercises of the musician—nothing more!

The aspirant must remember always that truth is living, changing, palpitating, and *cannot* be imprisoned in words. By attempting to state any aspect of truth he is at once caught in a lie! He must therefore seek that realm of thought where no words are, but where truth and power live, and from there he can radiate his influence outwards to touch the tendrils of his fellow men, which are reaching ever subconsciously to the highest and the best.

The aspirant must remember that if he can learn to realise and to use his power and influence from the subtler planes the world is his! Nothing can withstand such influence, and he can begin in silence to conquer, to create, and to work under guidance from Christ and His Hierarchy here on earth.

The author wishes to pay tribute to the following books for many of the statements and theories quoted in these chapters:

The Secret Doctrine, by H. P. BLAVATSKY.
A Treatise on the Seven Rays, by ALICE A. BAILEY.
The Rosicrucian Cosmo-Conception, by MAX HEINDAL.
From Sphinx to Christ, by EDOUARD SCHURÉ. (Rider.)
Creative Energy, by I. MEARS and L. E. MEARS. (John Murray.)
The Secret of the Golden Flower ('On Chinese Wisdom'), by WILHELM and JUNG. (Kegan Paul.)
An Outline for Boys, Girls and Their Parents (Science, Astronomy, etc.). (Gollancz.)
The Mystical Qabalah, by DION FORTUNE.
The Story of Psychic Science, by HEREWARD CARRINGTON. (Rider.)
The Secret of Life, by GEORGES LAKHOVSKY (Science). (Heinemann.)